# CHILDREN INDIAN CAPTIVES

By

Roy D. Holt

*Drawings By S.J. Stout*

---

EAKIN PRESS ★ BURNET, TEXAS

Copyright © 1980
By Roy D. Holt

Published in the United States of America
By Eakin Press, P.O. Box 178, Burnet, Texas 78611

ALL RIGHTS RESERVED

ISBN 0-89015-

# INTRODUCTION

These are true stories of boys and girls of another generation who rode horseback, for long or brief periods, with the greatest horsemen in history, the nomadic Indians of the Great Plains. All of the stories have Texas and the Southwest as their setting. Many of the stories are tragic. All depict the hazards of life on the western frontier. Courage, heroism, endurance, are to be found—along with carelessness and foolhardiness.

For countless decades, hard-riding Indian horsemen raided white settlements all over the vast Southwest, stealing horses, kidnapping white children and women, and murdering any unfortunate or unwary victim who crossed their trail. These horse raids were often endurance tests, even for seasoned warriors who from their earliest youth had spent their waking hours on the back of a spirited horse. Sometimes these horse-stealing expeditions lasted only for days, but they might extend for weeks or, in the case of one Comanche raid into Mexico, last for as long as two years. To the Plains Indians, horses were a medium of exchange and a quick barter commodity. Wealth to the Indians was in terms of ponies. Horse stealing, which was universal over the West, became a game, highly rewarding and vastly exciting. The most skillful and daring horse thief of the tribe was endowed with the highest possible honors. An Indian youth was, above all else, taught to ride a horse and steal horses without getting caught.

Usually the expert horse thieves slipped into the frontier settlements during the full of the moon. Isolated homes and small settlements were favorite targets. Horses were rounded up, day and night, until a sufficient number had been herded together. Then the Indian raiders drove their "catch" out of the country and to their main encampment. If the settlers pursued closely, the Indians rode day and night, hour after hour, even changing mounts on the run. This sometimes continued for hundreds of miles, or until the thieves were out of the danger zone.

Children and women taken captive by these fierce horsemen were often held for ransom or else made virtual slaves. Many, however, were adopted into the tribe, having become thoroughly "Indianized." The unfortunate captives when first caught were mounted on horses and forced to ride horseback with the Indians on their homeward endurance test. Since Indian youths could ride any horse, at any time, the savages expected their young captives to do the same. The more the captives suffered on the wild ride, the greater the satisfaction to many of the savage captors. This never-ending frontier war between the settlers and the Indians, age old in American history, was never a "sissy" game. A hated enemy prisoner has seldom been pampered in war-time, and frontier captives were "prisoners of war" to the Indians.

Since ancient days, mankind has used the horse as his best and fastest transportation. It is only in this century that man-made machines and inventions, still gauged in "horse power," has elevated man's faithful servant and beast of burden to uses of pleasure. Indeed, the horse is on the way back today and modern youth rides and observes the horse in parades, rodeos, riding clubs, racing, etc. while preceding generations knew the horse for his utility.

Also, now that machines and gadgets have made life far easier for the modern youth, it might be of some interest perhaps to compare our present blessings and comforts with the hardships of some youths who lived in the Southwest back when captives rode horseback with Indians who "were born on a horse."

\* \* \* \* \*

# CONTENTS

1. The Smith Boys Learned To Ride Like Indians . . . . . . . . . . . . 1
2. Ole Nystel Forced to Become a Horseman . . . . . . . . . . . . . . . 5
3. Cousins Had Horse Shot From Under Them . . . . . . . . . . . . . . 9
4. The Boy Who Rode With The Indian's Head . . . . . . . . . . . . 10
5. Dott Babb Rode The Comanche Race Horses . . . . . . . . . . . . 11
6. Tamasco, The Captive Mexican Girl . . . . . . . . . . . . . . . . . . . 15
7. Boy of 12 Never Returned From Indian Captivity . . . . . . . . 17
8. Tito Rivera Spent Three Years With The Comanches . . . . . 18
9. Young Widow Suffered Horrors Of Captivity . . . . . . . . . . . 19
10. Black Youth Showed Courage . . . . . . . . . . . . . . . . . . . . . . . 23
11. Frank Buckelew Was Proud To Be An American . . . . . . . . 24
12. Lipans Traded Boy For A Pony And Firewater . . . . . . . . . . 27
13. John Sowell Fought Indian Boy To Settle Horse Wager . . . 28
14. John O'Neal Rode Horseback For A Hundred Years . . . . . 31
15. Herman Lehmann Became Indianized . . . . . . . . . . . . . . . . 33
16. Indians Kidnap Freckled-Faced Boy At School . . . . . . . . . 38
17. Children Stolen By Indians In Austin . . . . . . . . . . . . . . . . . 41
18. Willie Lehmann Rode Six Days As An Indian Captive . . . . 42
19. Pete Johnson Used Ox Whip On The Comanches . . . . . . . 47
20. Tehan, The Red Headed Kiowa Warrior . . . . . . . . . . . . . . . 50
21. Pedro Espinosa, Boy Captive of the Comanches . . . . . . . . 51
22. Temple Friend Was "Indianized" . . . . . . . . . . . . . . . . . . . . 53
23. The Jackson Children Rode With Indian Horse Thieves . . 57
24. Williams Girl Stolen In Brown County . . . . . . . . . . . . . . . . 59
25. Riggs Girls Had Brief But Memorable Captivity . . . . . . . . . 60
26. Adolph Kohn, Captured While Herding Sheep . . . . . . . . . 63
27. Martha Virginia Webster Wrote of Her Tribulations . . . . . 63
28. Indians Took The German Sisters From Kansas . . . . . . . . . 67
29. The Mystery Of Johnnie Ledbetter . . . . . . . . . . . . . . . . . . . 72
30. Bosque John Learned White Man's Ways . . . . . . . . . . . . . 77
31. Coryell Youth Had Brief Ride With Brutal Redskins . . . . . 82
32. Texas Ranger Had Been Comanche Captive . . . . . . . . . . . 83
33. Young Woman From Texas . . . . . . . . . . . . . . . . . . . . . . . . . 87

# 1. Smith Boys Learned To Ride As Only Indians Could Ride

Clinton and Jeff Smith were herding sheep near their home at Dripping Springs, Texas, in 1869, when about twenty-five mounted Indians cut them off from the house. Clinton took his younger brother on his back and ran toward a cave but the Indians gave chase and surrounded the boys. Clint ran under one horse entirely, under the neck of another, and might have escaped into the brush but saw that his brother was being threatened with guns and tomahawks. The chief took Clint up on his horse behind him. The cavalcade passed near enough to the Smith home for the boys to see their mother and sisters standing on the front porch of the cabin. It was a sad farewell for the family.

The boys, like most of those who lived on the frontier, had simply become accustomed to the danger of Indian raids. Their father had been in numerous skirmishes with the red horse thieves. In fact, Indians had made five unsuccessful attempts to steal one or more of the nine Smith children. Clinton had escaped from the savages more than once, by hiding behind large rocks or climbing trees. Another time he and his brother were on horseback looking after the cattle when some seventy-five Indians found the boys. Their horses simply out ran those of the Indians, only to come to a raging stream at flood stage that must be crossed. The faithful horses carried the boys across to safety.

The red captors began their usual hasty exit away from the white settlements, riding hour after hour. The two boys were almost dead when the first stop was made. Here the savages killed a cow and ate the meat raw. When Clint refused to eat, an Indian pushed his head into the entrails. On the third day the Indians again killed a cow and the starving boys ate some of the raw liver, with the Indians laughing at them. The Indians roped a wild horse and made signs for Clint to mount. The boy tried to tell the savages that he couldn't ride that horse, without a saddle anyway. The savages were in a hurry to move on. The one holding the horse grabbed a stick of wood and struck Clint on the head, knocking him down. When the boy arose, the Indian again motioned him to mount. Clint climbed on the horse, which the Indians were holding, and then Jeff was placed behind Clint and both boys were tied to the horse. The horse was then turned loose and driven with the herd of stolen horses. Luckily the horse did not pitch or run away but the boys took a beating when the horses traveled through the brush. Near Fredericksburg, the Indians stole some saddled horses at a ranch house. One of the Indians was thrown by one of these horses. The

Indian was not accustomed to the white man's saddle. The other Indians caught the horse and the same rider crawled back on and this time rode the horse.

The red horse thieves continued to move westward, traveling all night and sometimes hiding all the day. They passed near Fort Concho and began to see plenty of buffalo. The Indians now slowed down, thinking that there was little danger of pursuit. Some of the Indians roped a young buffalo, tied the animal down, placed both the Smith boys on the animal's back, and then turned it loose. The Indians danced with delight at the sight of the white boys trying to stay with the buffalo. Clint was pitched off, but his younger brother clung like a cat. The buffalo began to run about in a wide circle and when Clint ran out to help his brother, the buffalo ran over him and knocked him down. The Indians finally roped the buffalo again and let the boy dismount.

When the boys were finally taken to the main Indian camp, they had a cruel initiation to face. Clint got into a fight with an Indian boy and was lucky enough to have a chief take his side. The chief wagered many horses that Clint could win the next fight. The boy tried every trick he knew, finally bit his opponent, and won. The chief then took the white boy as his son and gave him the name "End-of-a-Rope." One of his main duties was to guard the chief's horse herd at night. With the Indian boys, he swam, ran horse races, roped and rode horses all the time. Clint became an expert rider and roper, a skill he used all the remainder of his life. He rode in races, tied fast to the horse.

The Indians were always on the move. They ranged to the Rocky Mountains, to Montana, and back to Texas. Clinton saw many Mexican traders come to the Comanches, with pack-mules laden with coffee, sugar, tobacco, and ammunition. The Comanches traded their stolen horses and mules with little regard for the actual value.

Clinton took care of the chief's war, or buffalo, horse, an especially fast animal. The boy often rode a big mule that could run like a horse. While riding this mule, he killed his first buffalo with a spear. Clint also went on more than one horse stealing raid with the Indians. It was constant riding day and night. Clint rode a clumsy old saddle, something like a pack-saddle, and great sores were rubbed on his body. Finally, his horse gave out and the boy was so dead for sleep that he and his horse were caught in a buffalo stampede. Clint wounded a buffalo cow, which turned and knocked the poor horse down on top of Clint. The horse died, with Clint still under his neck. Further along the trail, the Indians captured many wild horses. A beautiful buckskin, with black mane and tail, was roped and Clint forcibly placed on his back and then tied on. Clint always remembered that horse as the worst pitching horse he ever rode. The animal pitched until he was exhausted and, after a short rest, began to run. Clint slipped under the horse's belly and it was a miracle that he was not kicked to death by the wild horse. The Indians watched the whole show and laughed hilariously. Finally, they took pity on the exhausted boy and his mount, roped the horse, and released Clint.

One time Clint was removing the pack saddle from an old mule when it turned under the animal, which started to pitch and kick. Clint held on to the rope for a time but then had to let go. A small keg of whiskey in the pack was kicked in and thus spilled. An old squaw ran to Clint and struck at him with her tomahawk. He dodged just in time to save his life, but she cut him badly on the hand.

After a time, Jeff Smith was traded to Apaches in New Mexico and the boy spent several years with them. They gave him the name "Horse-tail." The savages once forced Jeff to ride a big buck antelope, which they had hemmed up and roped. The boy was thrown time after time but forced to try again. Jeff finally locked his arms around the antelope's neck but again was thrown over the animal's head. This time, however, Jeff's belt hung on the antelope's horns. Jeff was badly bruised by the sharp hoofs of the pawing animal. An old squaw had been the cause of this ride, as she stood on the sidelines. Jeff got even with her later by cutting the girth of her saddle almost in two. He watched her saddle a wild mule, which was held by the ear, then mount. About the second jump the squaw and saddle sailed into space—and it was Jeff's turn to laugh.

Finally, both the Smith boys were returned to their home. When Clint was seventeen, he started out to get a job. Here his training as an Indian rider proved of some value to him. On his first job, he was given an old outlaw Zebra-striped horse to ride. He did!

Clinton Smith, trained in the hard school of Comanche horsemanship, rode that pitching horse to a finish. He gave the Indians credit for his skill as a rider. He always liked to tell about the ride for in time that old outlaw became his main mount. He told that the horse had been ridden so much that he stood still while the boy blindfolded and mounted him. When the blind was removed, the horse went straight up, came down facing the other direction with a jarring thud, and bawled like a calf. He tried all his tricks, which had unseated many a rider. He pitched over an acre of ground, but the boy stayed with him. Clint always declared that the horse tried everything on him but talk Spanish.

## 2. Ole Nystel Spent Three Months As Indian Captive

Ole Nystel, fourteen year-old boy living in the Norwegian colony in Bosque County, Texas, went out one morning with a companion to cut wood. A band of Comanches caught the boy away from his companion and shot him in the leg with an arrow. The companion, also badly wounded, ran several miles to his home. The Indians took the boy to their camp and offered him roasted horse meat. He refused it.

The savages began a long series of abuses and tortures for the boy. The pain from his wounded leg was almost unbearable but one of the savages grabbed the limb and twisted and wrenched it. The Indians kicked the helpless youth just for past-time and beat his bare back until it was bloody. All of his clothes were taken from him. If the boy fell asleep, the savages fired pistols so close to his face that he was badly burned and bore the scars the rest of his life.

When the marauders moved out, Ole was placed bareback on a poor, bony horse. The Indians rode at a gallop or trot mile after mile. Ole was forced to see other unfortunate victims fall into the clutches of the fiends. Some were tortured and murdered and the boy was made to laugh at their suffering, expecting his own death at any second. The Indians killed a calf and ate the meat raw. Ole was nauseated by the sight. The calfskin was placed on Ole's horse, flesh side up, and the boy made to remount. The weather turned bitterly cold. One of the Indians had the decency to give the naked, freezing boy the old overcoat which his companion had left when he escaped from the Indians. This saved Ole's life, he always believed.

It was on the ninth day after capture before Ole ate anything. In time he learned to eat everything, even raw meat. Not only did the boy suffer from lack of food and clothing, but his wound gave much pain and often he had a high fever.

On the trip back to their main camp, the Indians came to a large lake of water. The thirsty horses waded into the water to drink. Ole was mounted on a mule that did not want to leave when the other animals did. One of the savages rode near the mule, placed a pistol near the animal's ear and fired. The mule fell dead and Ole was dumped into the cold water on his head. The Indians dragged the freezing boy from the water and mud, threw him across the back of a horse like they would a sack of meal and hurried on their way. At another lake, the boy was put to digging roots with only his bare hands to serve as tools. His fingers became so numb that he stopped to rest. One of the Indians knocked him into the water. By this time the boy was becoming desperate. When he came out of the water he hit the Indian and knocked him down. Then he made the mistake of running. The Indian mounted a horse and caught the boy.

Once in the main Indian camp, Ole suffered through the torture of initiation by the squaws and children. He showed enough fight to win the grudging respect of the Indians after so long and he was given the job of herding horses. From then on his life was more bearable. He had seldom ridden horseback before, as did the typical Texas boy, but he soon became a good rider. With the Indian boys he rode much, ran horse races, and learned much horse lore. Ole also attracted the attention of the chief who had the boy prepare his coffee, when he had any. The chief's recipe for good coffee was to mix two cups of coffee with one of sugar.

Ole stole one of the fastest horses and managed to escape from the Indian camp one night. His horse gave out and the Indians again took Ole prisoner. When the redskins came up to him this time, he was laughing as if his running away was a big joke. The Indians did not laugh—but neither did they beat him. Soon after that the boy was forced to play a war game with the savages. Twenty mounted warriors lined up facing an equal number, all armed with bows and arrows. Ole was made to ride his pony at full speed between the two lines while they fired arrows a the moving target. Ole ran his gauntlet five or six times. He was not touched, nor was his horse, but three warriors were killed.

Ole related one incident which well illustrated the Comanche ability to ride a horse, for even the squaws were experts at this. The Indians had caught a small bear cub and when they started to move camp, the cub was placed in a sack and tied on the back of a pony and behind a squaw rider. A very severe cloud caused the Indians to hurry to a certain camping place. In the mad race to reach the spot before the storm broke, the bear cub no doubt was getting a terrific pummeling on the back of that galloping pony. The cub began to dig his claws into the horse's back in order to hold on. That pony did about everything—squealed, ran, jumped, kicked, pawed, reared on his hind legs, and finally went to bucking. The ferocious old squaw kept her seat through all that hub-bub without a trace of excitement. Ole took pity on the pony, the rider, and the cub. He raced his horse alongside, cut the rope, and let the cub drop to the ground.

Ole was ransomed by an Indian trader on the Arkansas River. He was gone from home six eventful months.

## 3. Captives Had Horse Shot From Under Them

Hiram Wilson and Diana Akers, cousins, both near their early teens were captured by Indians near their home in Parker County, Texas, in 1862. They had been sent to drive in the oxen but were caught by the Indians and each was forced to mount a horse, riding behind an Indian. Their harrowing ride with the marauders was about true to the usual pattern. The Indians stole more horses and rode day and night to get across the Red River with their plunder. The girl cried all the time. Both captives expected to be killed at any minute. After a brief rest, the boy and girl were tied to the back of an old roan mare and the animal was turned loose and driven with the herd. On the third day, the Indians made a brief stop and scorched some beef, which the starving children could eat sparingly.

The Indians were traveling at night and were near the present town of Ranger when a volley of shots was fired into the band. The Indians disappeared at once but several horses in the herd were killed, including the old roan upon which the children were mounted. The firing continued and more horses were killed around the boy and girl, who were on the ground and tied to a dead horse. Finally, the pair yelled so much that the attacking party, rangers and settlers, quit firing. These captives were fortunate indeed in being rescued so quickly. They were restored to their homes—with enough Indian experience to last a lifetime.

## 4. Rode With An Indian's Severed Head

Sam and Jim Savage were captured by a band of horse-stealing Indians near Weatherford, in 1866. One of the things that stood out in their memory of the whole miserable existence while held captive was the gruesome story of the severed head. One of the Indian riders was thrown from his horse (an unusual happening), in the fight in which the boys were captured. His body was caught in a rope tied to the horse's neck. The frightened animal ran, dragged the Indian several miles, and entirely severed the head from the Indian's body by being caught between rocks along the trail. A squaw in the raiding party carried that head in her lap on the whole trip back to the Indian Territory. The younger Savage boy had good reason to remember the whole thing—he too was carried in that squaw's lap along with the severed head.

Finally, a white trader bartered with the Indians and secured the release of the two boys. He gave to the Indians a silver-trimmed saddle, a bridle and a good horse. At long last the boys were restored to their parents. Besides the memories of their horrible experiences, the boys came to have a sort of a mania for saddles and horses. The reason? These were the objects which had secured their release from captivity. Also, the boys never had much hankering for Indian-head coins.

## 5.    Dot Babb Rode Comanche Race Horses

Death, flight, or capture were the alternatives faced by youth on the Texas frontier during Dot Babb's boyhood. Dot saw all of these in operation by fiendish Comanches.

When Dot was thirteen, he and his nine year-old sister saw a band of some thirty-five or forty painted Comanches as they swooped down and surrounded the Babb home in Wise County. This was in 1865 or 1866, when there was little protection for settlers on the frontier. Dot and his sister ran into the house and gave the alarm to his mother and to the only other occupant of the house, Mrs. Mary Ann Luster, a young widow. The door to the house was barred and Dot and his mother prepared their old guns for use, but the savages quickly broke down the door and overpowered their victims. Mrs. Luster took refuge in the loft. Mrs. Babb resisted and in trying to protect her family was stabbed four times and then shot with an arrow through the lungs. Dot was beaten over the head with quirts, overpowered, and dragged from the house. He saw that his mother was dying and he saw the Indians drag his sister and Mrs. Luster to the front of the house and mounted on horses, each behind an Indian rider.

Dob Babb later described those terrible moments: "An eternity of horror crowded into a moment of insufferable expense for unprotected and undefended women and children, confronted by merciless and remorseless savages."

Dot was also forced to mount behind an Indian, who held his hands tightly. All the horses in the area were rounded up and the thieves started their usual marathon race toward the Red River. The few pauses for rest and for changing horses were brief—no food and no sleep for the helpless captives. After crossing the Red River, there was some respite for the sufferers. The party camped and began to move on more leisurely. The watch over the captives was noticeably relaxed.

In camp on the Canadian River, Dot and Mrs. Luster made plans for escape. Dot was able to stake out a good horse that he knew had great speed and he knew that a certain mare would stay with the horse. That night the Indians bedded down in a great circle, with the three captives in the middle. Mrs. Luster awakened Dot and the two slipped carefully between the sleeping Indians. Dot's little sister had to be left behind. The main thing was to see that Mrs. Luster escaped from the savages, for by this time it was certain that the Comanche leader was planning to take her as his wife. Mrs. Luster reached the horse, fashioned a bridle out of the stake rope, mounted and waited for Dot. Before the boy could secure the mare, the Indians came running. Dot told the young widow to ride for her life. She did just that.

Dot slipped back to his bed in the Indian circle and was elated to note that it was at least an hour before the escape of Mrs. Luster was detected. Several of the Indians took up the pursuit of Mrs. Luster, while the others began a plan of diabolical torture for the Babb captives. Dot was placed against a big tree and several Indians took their stand some twenty yards away with bows, arrows and pistols. They made signs that they were going to riddle Dot's body. His sister was forced to witness the torture. She began to cry loudly, and Dot talked to her and tried to soothe her. Several Indians then stepped between the boy and his tormentors, only to be pushed aside roughly. Dot was then bound with a rawhide rope and tied to a stake. The Indians began to collect dry grass and brush and pile it around the boy. The sister again began to wail and weep. Instead of setting fire to the prisoner, the Indians held a council at the conclusion of which Dot was untied and told, "Heap bueno you!" Dot's lack of fear had saved his life.

When the raiding party reached the main Comanche camp, Dot began an active but not always pleasant life. He spent sixteen months with this band of Nocona Comanches. At first he was put to work helping the squaws around the camp. The squaws and the Indian children abused him until one day he asserted his rights and fought back. After that he began to play with the boys and to help with the horses. "I joined the Indian boys in catching, riding, and breaking wild horses, which was an exciting sport and an excellent past time," declared Dot in his book, *In The Bosom Of The Comanches.*

Chief Pernerney, a bold and daring warrior, claimed Dot as his property. One of the chief's stunts was to arm Dot with an old cap and ball six-shooter and force him to shoot at the chief, who on horseback would dash past the boy. The Comanche proudly demonstrated that he could catch every bullet on his buffalo bullhide shield.

But is was to Chief Asahavey (Dot spelled it Esserhaby) that Dot paid respectful tribute. It was this chief who was responsible for restoring the Babb children to their father. In fact, Asahavey restored many white captives to their homes and worked untiringly to bring peace between the Comanches and the whites. Asahavey gave several fine horses, saddles, bridles, and blankets as a ransom to secure Dot's release and then started with the boy on a leisurely trip to Fort Arbuckle, there to meet his father.

The portion of Dot's stay with the Indians was the part that he liked to recall. He enjoyed the trip with Asahavey's tribe and he came to love the horse racing. The chief owned a number of race horses and was very shrewd in matching the races. Dot became his main jockey, and after winning six races out of six starts, the old chief wanted to keep him. Dot and the chief rode the horses all the time and knew exactly the speed of each horse and the best distance to run each. Whenever the Comanches came to an Indian camp, horse racing became the main object.

At length Dot and his sister were restored to the father, who repaid Asahavey the ransom price. In returning to Texas, after two years with the Comanches, Dot was almost drowned in the raging torrent of the Red River. He was riding a small black two-year-old horse, which stopped swimming in the main channel, turned on his side, and began to float downstream. The boy stayed with the pony and managed to get him to the Texas side. In later life, Dot worked with cattle and drove Longhorns up the trail to Kansas.

NOTE: In 1912, T. A. (Dot) Babb published his book, *In The Bosom Of The Comanches*. It vividly described the experiences of the captives. For some reason he used the name Luster for the young lady who escaped from the Indians, after being taken captive with the two Babb children. The contemporary Indian archives use the name of Sarah Roberts and her experiences are described later. The name Luster and Roberts are evidently for the same person.

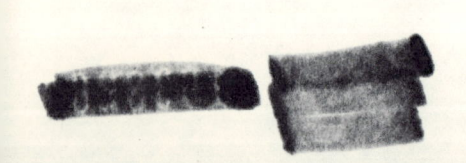

# 6.     Tamasco, Captive Mexican Girl

When a very young child, Tamasco was taken captive at her home in northern Mexico by Comanche Indians. She was taken by her captors into Texas, where she spent her childhood. When some of the Southern Comanches were placed on the Indian reservation in Young County in 1855, Tamasco attracted the attention of Indian agent Robert S. Neighbors. He faithfully tried to locate her people but in this had no success, since the girl could not remember her family name.

Some of the Comanches, fearing that they would lose their captive, took her into New Mexico and there bartered her to Comancheros, or Mexicans who traded regularly with the Comanches. The girl's new owners were so cruel to her, that she was determined to run away and return to the free roving life with the Indians. This was when she was about twelve years of age. She carefully made plans and bided her time. A ten-year old captive Indian was persuaded to make the break with her. The opportunity to flee came when the master was attending a religious festival. Tamasco and the boy mounted the one horse they could get, riding eastward into the vast Llano Estacado. A week later they were completely lost and were starving. In desperation, they killed their poor horse and ate the meat until the wolves and buzzards crowded them away. With strength somewhat revived, the fugitives walked until they literally dropped in their tracks, more dead than alive. But youth can rebound quickly.

Tamasco dreamed that about a mile to the north was a trail which would in turn fork a few miles farther on. The right fork would lead to an Indian encampment. At dawn, the pair found the trail and followed it to an Indian village. The fatigued pair were accepted by the Indians, fed generously, and finally became members of the tribe.

Tamasco felt right at home with the Indians, since

that was the only life she had known. A kind Indian woman adopted her as a daughter and cared for her until she was fourteen and a very attractive maiden. The mother thought she was old enough to marry and, in keeping with tribal custom, bartered her for horses to a man named Blue Legs. But Tamasco had not been consulted. When the bridegroom came to claim his squaw, Tamasco rebelled and told Blue Legs that she hated him and would never marry him. In a blind rage, she ran at the man, kicking and scratching. To further disgrace the warrior, she pulled his long plaits, ruffled his feathers, and smeared his war paint. The Indian brave made a hasty retreat. In despair the mother asked the girl whom she wanted to marry, for she must marry someone.

Tamasco immediately pointed to young Joseph Chandler, a halfbreed Comanche boy who had also lived on the Comanche reservation in Texas and had moved with his people into Indian Territory when all the reserve Indians were expelled from Texas in 1859. Young Chandler was flattered to be the choice of the attractive girl who had grown up since he had known her in Texas. He quickly asked Blue Legs what he would take for his proprietary interest in the girl. In disgust, the latter replied, "Three dollars and a crowing chicken!" Chandler met the price and the girl became his property. In respect to her youth, however, the Scotch-Indian placed the girl in the home of a white trader's family until she reached the age of seventeen, when the couple were married.

A few years later the Chandler family established their home near the Kiowa-Comanche agency on Cache Creek in Indian Territory. They raised a large family of children and their descendants are today respected citizens of Oklahoma. They also had the respect of the Indians, with whom they had always lived, and their influence proved very helpful to the army officers and Indian agents in their dealing with the Indians. The Chandlers became fast friends with Quaker agent Laurie Tatum and his wife. Agent Tatum told the story of Joseph and Tamasco in his diary.

## 7.    Boy of 12 Never Returned From Indian Captivity

A boy of 12, Frank Gephart, went out from the little village of Castroville one day with a grown man to hunt for some strayed oxen. They observed several men on horseback, all wearing hats, driving horses across the prairie. They naturally supposed that the men were settlers of that area. Their lack of care proved costly, for the riders proved to be Indians, who charged the pair yelling and shooting.

The man cautioned the boy not to be afraid because they were on good horses that could outrun those of the Indians. The race for survival began, with the man keeping between the boy and the Indians. The boy's horse came to a deep gully, refused to make the jump, and ran along it. The man shot at the Indians as they neared the boy, but they continued their charge, and showered arrows at the man. An Indian caught the bridle of the boy's horse and took Frank and his horse with them. The man managed to escape and organize a posse to follow the Indians. The boy was never seen nor heard of again by his family.

During the decade of the fifties and sixties, it was a saying on the frontier of Texas that at least one member of every family had been crippled, killed, or kidnapped by the Indians.

## 8. Tito Rivera Spent Three Years With Comanches

Tito Rivera, born in Mexico of wealthy parents, was captured by raiding Comanches when about ten years old. His father had permitted him to go with a party of men across the mountains to secure food for the miners. On the way home the Comanches took the boy and the sixty mules in the pack train. Tito always recalled vividly the long ride through northern Mexico and across Texas. It was adventure perhaps, but not to a homesick, weary boy.

After some three years of captivity, Tito was taken by some of the Comanches to the Texas Comanche Reservation, near Camp Cooper. In 1855, the United States Government paid $125 for the ransom of the boy. Indian agent Robert S. Neighbors tried to notify the boy's parents that he had been found but was unable to locate them.

Perhaps it was Tito Rivera who came to the camp of Captain R. B. Marcy with the Comanches once. The Captain asked the boy why he did not leave the Indians and go home to his own people. The boy replied that he had been so long among the Indians that he lied and stole horses just as good as any Indian.

Agent Neighbors took Tito to his own home in San

Antonio and kept the boy there until the former's death in 1859. For some time Tito then made his home with William A. Wallace (Big Foot). During the Civil War he served some time on the frontier ranger force and later with the Third Texas Cavalry. After the war, Tito entered the cattle business and made one trip up the trail, spending eighteen months on the trip. Later Tito settled at Corpus Christi and became a prominent citizen in the Gulf Coast area.

## 9. Young Widow Suffered Horrors Of Indian Captivity

One of the most gripping of all the stories concerning horrors of captivity among the Indians was that of Jane Wilson. At the age of fifteen, Jane Adeline Smith married James Wilson in Lamar County, Texas. In 1853, the young couple joined a wagon caravan bound for the California gold fields. Also in the party were Wilson's father and three small brothers.

Even the Texas portion of the trail was long and hazardous. In El Paso, the Wilsons had the misfortune to have their teams stolen and they could not continue with the wagon train. It was decided they would return to their old home. On the return trip, near the Guadalupe Mountains, both James Wilson and his father were killed by Indians. Jane and the three small boys hurried back to El Paso, crushed by the horrors already suffered. Before long, they were able to get attached to a small caravan returning to the settlements. This meant another trip entirely across Texas and practically every foot was in dangerous Indian country. A man named Hart was in charge of this wagon train and he succeeded in guiding the party through until, in the vicinity of Fort Phantom Hill, three of the teamsters deserted and drove away many of the Hart horses. Hart and the eldest Wilson lad pursued the runaways, leaving Jane Wilson, the other two Wilson boys and one Mexican with the stalled wagons. With the few horses left behind, this unprotected party started toward the Fort.

The hapless wayfarers rode into disaster almost at once. A band of Comanche warriors, whose sentinels had been spying upon the wagons, raced around the foot of a hill and surrounded the wagons. The Mexican was killed and scalped while the horrified Wilsons looked on helplessly. The scalp was crammed into the big sombrero worn by the Mexican, seized by one of the murderers, and placed on his own head. Jane and the two small boys were seized and thrown upon the backs of horses, then tied fast. In fiendish glee the savages ransacked the wagons, taking what they could carry. The wagon teams were cut loose from their harness and the party began a hard, long ride to get out of the country.

Wagon boss Hart returned to the scene of the capture, then hastened to Fort Phantom Hill to get aid. The commandant at that post favored a peace policy with the Comanches, some of whom were on a reservation on the Brazos at the time. He refused to take punitive steps toward the murderers but instead talked with some of the Comanche chiefs, gave them presents, and secured a promise that the chiefs would use their "influence" in recovering the captives. Nothing was done as a result.

Jane Wilson now was forced into an existence marked only by intense suffering, persecution, and torture. Captivity was bad enough for the two Wilson youths, but they soon came to enjoy all the outdoor activities of Indian life. Whenever the hard-riding savages made brief stops, the prisoners were bound and closely guarded. On the second day, during one stop, the plunder and the captives were distributed among the Indians. For twelve, long and horrible days, the captives were borne along on the horseback torture rack.

The unfortunate young widow was forced to ride an unbroken mule, without a bridle. The old saddle was a mere torture rack, and the jolting gait of the mule was unceasing misery. Frequently the mule would begin bucking and throw the girl over its head. The savages laughed each time and so the chief, to further gratify their malice, would shake the Mexican's bloody scalp before the mule's eyes. The terrified beast then would rear and plunge until the rider was flung violently to the ground. Some days she was thrown as many as a half-dozen times and once was so badly stunned that she could not arise for some time. The repeated falls brought heathenish peals of laughter from the Indians each time. If the hapless rider did not rise at once after each fall, the tormentors would beat her with their quirts, gunsticks, or the end of lariats. One squaw in the party jabbed the girl with the point of a spear many times.

To further add to the girl's utter misery, most of her clothing had been torn away and her long, flowing hair cut off with a butcher knife. The scorching sun blistered her body from head to toe. To move at all brought excruciating pain. But the worst of all her woes was that Jane expected to become a mother within a few weeks. The fiendish redskins understood her condition and thus planned their horrible torture, such as riding the wild mule. Not once did one of the savages show any sign of compassion to the girl. They seemed to study methods of putting her to death a little at a time.

In camp, Jane was forced to work like a slave, without a moment's rest. She was compelled to carry great loads of wood on her bare back which became a mass of blisters and sores. Blood ran down to her feet from her back. She had to herd the horses and mules through the briars and bushes, until what few clothes she still wore were torn to shreds. Each morning she had to drive the horses to camp and when a wild horse got away the savage chief knocked her down. She had to saddle her own mule each time without any assistance, and somehow, she and that mule could never be friends.

At length, the captors made the prisoners walk, with the mounted warriors following closely. Jane became so exhausted that she fell and the brutes forced their horses to trample upon her. The girl's feet became lacerated and bleeding. She had no rest and could sleep little at night. She still had to perform all the camp menial tasks and do the cooking for the entire party.

By unexpected but great good fortune, the girl managed to get on the trail in advance of the Indians one morning. She had hidden some food in a large hollow cottonwood tree, just in hopes that she could escape. Now she slipped through the bushes and hid in the hollow tree. Her captors searched the whole area but her luck held and finally the Indians moved on. The tree served as her home and hiding place for several days. She got water at a nearby spring and found wild berries to eat. When some Comancheros (Mexican traders with the Comanches) camped at the spring, Jane decided to take her chances and get them to rescue her. They treated her with kindness and finally took her to New Mexico. In due time she was restored to relatives in Texas.

In 1853, Indian traders went to a Comanche village on the Canadian River and learned that these Indians had a white boy, named George W. Wilson. The Comanche who claimed the boy refused to part with him under any consideration, saying that he was old and needed the boy to catch his horse for him. The chief of the tribe intervened and at last the boy was ransomed for many items of trade goods. The old chief for his services was given a pony, a rifle, and six plugs of tobacco. The traders then learned that George had a brother, Meredith, with another band of Comanches. George begged to take his younger brother's place as a captive. However, a Kickapoo trader located Meredith and ransomed him. The Congress of the United States, in 1854, appropriated $1,000 to repay the traders for their ransom money.

## 10.  Black Youth Showed Nerve

In Kerr County, a black boy about twelve years of age was sent to mill with some corn to be ground into meal. As he rode along on horseback, Indians surrounded him and made him captive. He knew that obedience was all that might save his life, but he tried not to show his fear. His very first initiation was a whipping with a quirt. This was followed by a ride of fully twenty-four hours without stopping. When they camped, one Indian threatened to cut the boy's throat. The boy remained calm and did not cry out. Several Indians yelled "bravo" to him and showed more respect after that. One bully did force the muzzle of his six-shooter into the boy's mouth but the victim again showed no fright.

The boy saw one peculiar thing happen while he was a captive of the red marauders. A little girl, about eight, had been stolen from her home near Center Point and was mounted one morning on a horse that pitched violently every time an Indian mounted. Strange to say, the vicious horse was as docile as a lamb for the girl. Soon an Indian mounted the horse and he pitched over a big area. Many old time Indian fighters in Texas affirmed that horses could smell Indians and some horses were decidedly "anti-Indian."

## 11. Frank Buckelew Was Proud To Be An American

Frank Buckelew, an orphan boy of twelve, and a black boy were sent out near their home on the Sabinal River to hunt some lost oxen. A big Indian ran the white boy down on foot and captured him but the black youth escaped and ran home to tell the tale. Frank was taken before the leader of the Indian raiding party, who in "broken" English and Spanish asked the boy if he was Americano or "Red beard" (German). If he was German, his life would be spared. The twelve-year-old boy did not hesitate and he did not lie. He told the chief that he was American, proud of it, could not help it if he wanted to, and then told the chief to do his "darndest." The chief was stumped by the answer.

The boy was then stripped of all his clothing and carried with the Indians as they covered the country stealthily in securing more horses. Sometimes Frank would be left alone for hours, securely bound, while all the Indians were out looking for more horses. At other times he would be forced to help catch and herd the horses already taken. The prickly pear thorns and the briers made his entire body so sore that he could barely move. One Indian knocked him down with a block of wood when he did not carry out an order quickly enough.

    The Indians at last went to a large encampment of the tribe on the Pecos River. His initiation was started by a squaw drawing a sharp butcher knife across his throat.

Frank was determined not to flinch or show fear. The warriors patted the boy on the back and said "Bravo! Bravo!" He stayed with the Comanches for eleven months, making several trips with them. On a trip into Mexico, it happened that a Texas rancher saw the boy, found out who he was, and finally helped him escape. Frank was sent back to his sisters at Bandera.

Frank Buckelew never forgot what he observed in the red riders. They had uncanny ability to catch and tame a wild horse. Their ability to ride a horse was little short of unbelievable. Of course their training started almost at birth and later every boy was made to ride bucking horses, just as the captive boys were given the same treatment.

Frank recalled his own initiation. Among the Lipans' horse herds was one small pony that could usually throw any rider, even a seasoned warrior, almost as soon as he was mounted. The pony was led to the camp, a brawny warrior seized Frank and placed him on the pony without bridle, rope or saddle. The horse was turned loose. Only a few jumps unseated the boy, threw him head-first to the ground and kicked him as he fell. Frank did not remember how long he stayed blacked out—but he always remembered that ride.

In *Texas Indian Papers, 1860-1916,* edited by James M. Day and Dorman Winfrey, frequent mention is made of the Buckalew case. In January of 1867, N.M.C. Patterson, County Judge of Uvalde County, wrote to Governor J. W. Throckmorton that W. B. Hudson of Kinney County had turned the boy captive, Frank Buckelew, over to him for judicial purposes. The story told in the letter was that Frank had been captured the year before and taken to the Lipan Indian encampment in Mexico. Hudson found out about the boy, hired a Mexican to induce him to run away while out herding the Indian horses. The Mexican and the boy selected good horses and managed to escape. The horses bore brands of Texas ranches.

The next month, H. I. Richarz of Castroville wrote to Governor Throckmorton describing the severity of the continuous raids made by Lipan and Kickapoo Indians from Mexico upon the settlers all over southwest Texas. Richarz stated that young Buckalew had just passed through that section after escaping from the Lipans and that the boy told that the Indians drove whole herds of cattle and horses out of Texas and into Mexico.

And in June of 1867, County Judge E. Orborske, of Bandera County, in a report to the governor of Texas gave a statement from "Francis Maryan Buckalew," who had lately returned from Indian captivity in Mexico. Frank described how the Lipan had taken him to the Pecos River and then into Mexico and how the Mexican (who would not give his name) had not only helped him escape but had accompanied him all the way to his relatives in Bandera County.

## 12. Lipans Traded Captive Boy For A Pony And Firewater

Not only did Comanche, Kiowa, and Apache Indians make raids in Mexico and Texas to steal horses and captives, but Indians from Mexico came into Texas to kill, kidnap, and plunder.

In 1864, about twenty Lipan Indians from Mexico surrounded the sheep camp of George Schwander and made captives of Mrs. Schwander and her six-year-old son, Albert. The father was absent at the time. The mother and son were forced to travel on foot, while most of the Indians were mounted. The desperate mother tried to escape and was murdered. The raiders kept moving until far into the night.

The frightened and bewildered boy was tied on a pony the next morning, being forced to ride behind a young Indian. The path of travel was westward and led across the Devil's River. Each night the boy was made to sleep between two warriors, who pinned him down with their arms. He was made to walk over rocky ground. His feet became so bruised and swollen that each step was torture. As was customary, the Indians tore the clothing from the boy and he suffered greatly from exposure. The only food was meat without salt and prickly pear apples. The diet made the boy sick. Once the Indians beat Albert because he could not catch the horses.

Albert's father and a party of white men followed the Indians and caught up with them long enough to engage them in a brief skirmish. The Indians got away with the stolen horses, however. At length, the Indians crossed the Rio Grande near El Paso and traded Albert to a Mexican for a pony and some "firewater." This master was kind enough to the boy and agreed later to return Albert to his father at a high price. Albert always remembered that adventurous trip but never had any desire to repeat it.

## 13. John Sowell Fought Indian Boy To Settle Horse Wager

John Sowell, at the age of thirteen, was driving the cows from the pasture one afternoon near his home in Fannin County, when two Indians caught him and hastily dragged him into the brush. The savages had several stolen horses tied nearby. One stood over the boy with a tomahawk while the other stripped him of every bit of his clothing, tied his hands tightly behind him, then flung him on a horse and tied his feet under the horse's belly.

The Indians rode hard to get out of the country, seldom pausing the first night and day. On the second night, the Indians stopped near a small creek, staked their horses, and built a fire. One of the savages killed a deer with his bow and arrow. The meat was roasted and eaten. They paid little attention to the boy, who lay on the ground, tied hand and feet.

John described his never-to-be-forgotten misery: "I was in a racking pain, being badly lacerated from riding horseback, and my back was burned and blistered from the hot rays of the sun."

The suffering lad could lie only on his stomach. He felt that he would never be able to move again. He could not sleep during the long night and his body was consumed with a high fever.

At daylight, the Indians forced meat into the boy's mouth, bruising and cutting his lips. Then they deliberately broke the blisters on his back, laughing fiendishly at his show of pain.

He was placed on a horse again and rode in a stupor. That day they met a larger band of Indians. The chief rode around the captive and, surprisingly, showed some compassion. He untied the boy's numb hands and placed a buffalo robe on the horse for John to use.

Upon reaching the main Indian camp, John became the target for the abuse of all the savages. The boys struck, kicked, and punched him with sharp sticks and arrows. An Indian squaw came to his rescue and by signs told him to fight back. He waded in and made it a free-for-all fight. The squaw dressed the boy's wounds and later made him some buckskin clothing.

After this the chief claimed John for his own property. The Indian practice of gambling was shown by the chief when he made a wager of one pony with another chief that John could whip his boy. Each boy was told that if he lost he would be whipped. Every Indian in the village gathered to watch and to wager and yell. It was a long and gory fight but John won. When his owner went to collect the pony, the two chiefs got into an argument and drew their knives to fight it out. The squaw who had befriended John stepped between them and spoke a few words. The loser delivered the pony he had wagered but in a fury beat the boy who had lost the fight.

John stayed with the Indians for nearly four years. His opponent in the fight became his best friend. They rode horses, played, swam, and hunted together. John spent much of his time with the horse herd and he became as expert as any Comanche boy when it came to handling a horse. But he never became really "Indianized" as did many white captives. Frequently he saw raiding parties return to the village with stolen horses and captives. It always made him sad to see the scalps of white victims hung to a pole in the center of the village. Finally the Comanches were forced to go to a reservation and their captives and their horses taken from them. At the age of seventeen, John was finally restored to his father, who did not recognize the boy at first.

S.J. Stout

## 14. John O'Neal Rode Horse Back For A Hundred Years

John O'Neal at the age of 106 was riding horseback every day, thus rounding out more than a century in the saddle. At an early age he became an orphan and went to live with his uncle, who taught him how to shoot a gun, ride any horse and handle cattle. At the age of eleven he was doing the work of a man in riding the range and was the proud owner of his own horse and saddle. John's favorite story was his own experience as a captive with the Indians for some five years.

John had a good pony and, boy like, was absolutely certain that this pony could outrun any horse in the country. In spite of many warnings given to the boy about Indian dangers, he felt no fear whatever when mounted. He knew that he could outrun any or all of them. In fact, he came to the decision that he would welcome meeting some Indians so that he could show them up. Gradually each day he rode a little farther away from his companions.

One day when alone on the prairie, John saw an Indian riding toward him. John let the red rider get within some 300 yards and then started to race away. He kept looking back at the pursuing lone Indian. When he saw the gap between them widen, he kept looking back and laughing. What he had failed to see, to his regret, was a second Indian mounted on a fast horse and riding to cut across the boy's path. John's pony tired quickly and the Indians caught the boy and made him captive.

During the next five years, John was an Indian to all outward appearances. He lived the nomadic life of the Indian boy, riding horses much of the time. At first he did menial tasks about the camp but as he seemed to please the chief he was soon herding horses and even going on hunts with the warriors. He learned to speak Comanche and Spanish.

John became close friends with an old Mexican captive named Juan. The boy wanted to run away from the Indians but the Mexican urged patience and the two began to make plans for the boy's escape. John was to take his pony a little farther from camp each day and after a time he asked the old chief if he could have his saddle. The chief granted this permission and John continued to ride, but came back to camp just a little later each day. Finally,

John announced to Old Juan that he could not stand captivity any longer. He was leaving that very night. To his delight the old Mexican announced that he was going along.

That night in the intense darkness, the pair slipped from the Comanche village, secured their horses, and led them slowly out of camp. John wanted to mount and make a run for freedom, but old Juan held them to a snail's pace, even after they had mounted and had traveled more than a mile without hearing any pursuit. After what seemed hours, old Juan said, "Now, we ride hard!" And it was a ride, indeed. After many miles, John's horse gave out but luckily Juan located a house with horses in a corral. Two fresh horses were taken from the corral and the fugitives resumed their race. When they came to a stream, they tried to hide their trail by following the stream. They rode continually for two nights and one day and then they began to rest during the day. After many days they rode up to the front of a house and Juan shouted. John did not recognize the place until his uncle came to the door. A joyful reunion took place, with the Uncle offering old Juan one thousand dollars in gold for the safe return of the nephew. Later, John rode as a Texas Ranger, as an Indian fighter, and as a cattle owner and rancher thus rounding out a hundred years on horseback.

## 15. Herman Lehmann Spent Nine Years With The Apaches And Comanches

Herman Lehmann's parents came from Germany, in 1846, and suffered all the vicissitudes of taming the frontier. In 1870, the family was living some twenty-five miles northwest of Fredericksburg. Herman was eleven at the time. Herman, nine year-old Willie, and two small sisters were sent by the mother one day to drive the birds from a wheat field near the house. The father was absent at the time. Suddenly a large band of mounted Indians rode up near the field. Two of them dismounted and caught the four children, after quite a chase. The two captors tried to cross the fence some distance from their mounted comrades. The two boys put up such a struggle that the Indian holding the girls threw them over the fence and went to the aid of the other redskin. The little girls ran toward the house for dear life, urged on by their frantic mother's cries. The mounted Indians gave chase right up to the yard gate, and discharged arrows toward their intended victims. The intrepid mother stood in the yard with a shotgun and defied the Indians to come nearer. The little girls reached the house unhurt.

Herman and his brother, with sinking spirits, saw the whole chase until the little girls reached safety. Both boys were securely tied and placed on horseback. The marauders left in a hurry. A few miles farther the band camped and killed a calf for food. The stomach was removed and the milk contained in it was devoured with great relish by the Indians. The entrails were offered to the boys and, when they refused to partake, Herman was seized by a burly savage and the boy's head was thrust into the paunch. Both boys were then forced to eat some of the warm, bloody liver. The captives were then stripped of all their clothing and the band started rapidly on their way with their stolen horses. The boys became sun-burned over their entire bodies. But there was no relief in sight. The harrowing ride, hunger, and loss of sleep made their misery complete.

Willie, who was not tied, managed to escape from the Indians one night and after days of intense suffering the boy made his way back to the San Saba River. Two ranchmen found him there and returned him to his home.

Herman was taken to the Apache village in New Mexico. Here he steeled himself against savage taunts and insults. He fought back and came to be accepted by the Indians. Gradually he became an Indian boy, living an untrammeled life generally. Sometimes his master beat him unmercifully but he rode with other Indian boys. He learned to use the bow and arrow and the lasso. He herded horses and learned to ride so well that he was taken on horse stealing raids with a band of Apaches. The Texas Rangers caught the raiders in the vicinity of San Angelo and a sharp skirmish ensued. Herman fired arrows at the Rangers as rapidly as he could. He saw a horse go down and saw an Indian running for dear life. Herman dashed alongside the fleeing Indian and took him behind him on the horse. Soon however the horse was killed by a ranger bullet and Herman was pinned to the ground by the dead horse. The other Indian grabbed Herman's bow and ran away, only to be run down and killed. Herman worked frantically to extricate himself and when he succeeded, crawled through the high grass and hid. The Rangers returned and spent an hour looking for him but finally gave up and left the scene. Herman was in some predicament. As the sole Indian survivor, he was 300 miles from the Indian village, which he now called home. He was afoot, without food, and unarmed. On the long lonely journey he almost starved. He ate prickly pear, grasshoppers, and anything that he could find. Since he had no way of carrying water, his thirst almost drove him mad at times. But make it he did, reaching the Apache encampment so exhausted that it took a long time for him to recover. The Indians showed kindness usually not attributed to the savages. Herman's prestige in the tribe brought their respect.

One of the Apache chiefs, who had been shot by Mrs. Lehmann during another raid on the frontier home, bore a grudge against the boy and showed that he was planning to kill him. One day Herman was herding the large "caballada" of horses and some of the horses got away from him. A number of the strayed horses belonged to the hated chief, who immediately came looking for the herder. Herman fled, took refuge on a rocky hill, and killed the chief by shooting an arrow through his body. Herman hid until darkness came and then he slipped into the village and went to the lodge of his foster parents. The couple, with praise-worthy courage and sincere love for the boy, prepared him for flight. They carried food, a canteen of water, bow and arrows, saddle, lasso, and blanket to a designated hiding place. They were powerless to do more. The foster father told Herman to catch a certain horse from the herd, one known for his stamina, and ride day and night. The old squaw cried bitterly when she told the boy goodbye.

Herman caught the horse he wanted and was soon riding eastward. When the sun came up, he was on a vast waterless plain. The journey continued all day. The horse suffered for water until late in the afternoon, they came to a creek. Herman staked the horse so that he could graze and then climbed on the top of a high ridge from which he could see moving objects in the distance, mere specks, but he knew that the Apaches were on his trail. Herman hastily remounted and pushed on. Many days of harrowing travel followed, with horse and rider almost perishing from hunger and thirst. Herman was leading the exhausted horse when they came to a wide, deep canyon with a stream of clear flowing water and good grass. Here Herman lived for several months, finding shelter in a cave and plenty of game for food. His constant dread was that some nomadic Indians would find him and either kill him or return him to the Apaches.

One night the boy heard human voices, the first in months, and he discovered that a band of Indians had made a camp a few hundred yards away. To his dismay, he found they were Apaches. He mounted his horse and fled. He did not know where he was going but he knew he must keep moving. At length he came to a vast region destitute of grass and water and the weather had turned bitterly cold. He saw a band of Indians about a mile away preparing to make camp. He waited until darkness came, then went to the camp and boldly walked into the midst of the surprised Indians. The warriors jumped to their feet and surrounded the boy, who soon learned that he was among the Comanches. These Indians treated him with kindness during the five years he lived with them. In time he was adopted into the tribe and went to the reservation in Indian Territory when the Comanches were forced to give up their roving life.

Herman always remembered one wild ride he made while living with the Indians. The warriors captured a large fat mustang stallion and tied him down. Herman was securely tied to the animal, which was blindfolded. With Indians mounted on swift horses placed in a circle around the wild horse, the stallion was released. The first thing he did was to look around and bite Herman on the arm. Herman forgot that he was an Indian just then and gave a lusty yell. This seemed to start the horse on a zig-zag course, pitching and running. The animal came to a deep ditch and cleared it at one bound but the other Indian horses could not cross it. The horse ran for at least ten miles and passed from sight of the Indian horseman. At length, he came to another deep gully and tried to leap it. The seemingly exhausted animal fell to his knees and Herman was thrown over his head. The wild mustang was not tired at all, judging from his actions. Herman lay on the ground and saw the horse jump to his feet and race away as smoothly as he had done the first mile. Herman was not hurt by the fall but his arm was giving him agonizing pain. When the pursuing riders finally came up, they gave the boy cheers and laughed heartily. They bound up his arm and took the boy back to camp.

Herman Lehmann came to love the life of the Indian. He learned to do everything on a horse that a Comanche could do. He became a jockey of repute among the Comanches, riding many races tied to the horse. More than once he suffered the misfortune of slipping under the horse's belly, but always came out unhurt.

Herman Lehmann was restored to his home after nine

years of Indian life. Some of his experiences were later recorded in his book, *Nine Years With The Indians*. He died in 1935.

## 16. Indians Kidnap Freckled-Faced Boy At School

In the Indian archives of Texas, a communication from the sheriff of Hamilton County reads:

"June 67 Ind killed Miss Whitney—carried off a boy." And also among the musty records is a letter from J. S. White, County Judge of Hamilton, dated July 11, 1867, to Governor J. W. Throckmorton stating that, after the Indian attack on the school house, the savages "captured and carried off a little boy of the following description and name John M. Kuykendall aged 8 years auburn hair fair complexion and very freckled."

Miss Ann Whitney was the teacher in a little one-room log school house on the Leon River in Hamilton County, in the summer of 1867. Some of the pupils saw Indians some distance from the school house. The teacher barred the one door and aided her charges to crawl through a window and escape into the brush along the river bank—that is, nearly all the students. Two small boys were hidden underneath the floor boards and two small girls stayed with the teacher.

The hideously painted savages quickly surrounded the house and fired arrow after arrow through the cracks between the logs. With blood streaming from multiple wounds, the heroic teacher continued to walk from one side of the room to the other trying to protect the little girls and pleading for their lives. All the Indians soon gathered at the door and attempted to batter it down. Ann Whitney, making a last supreme effort, helped the small girls to escape through the back window. The door gave way and the savages had to push aside the body of the teacher in order to enter. The frontier teacher had made

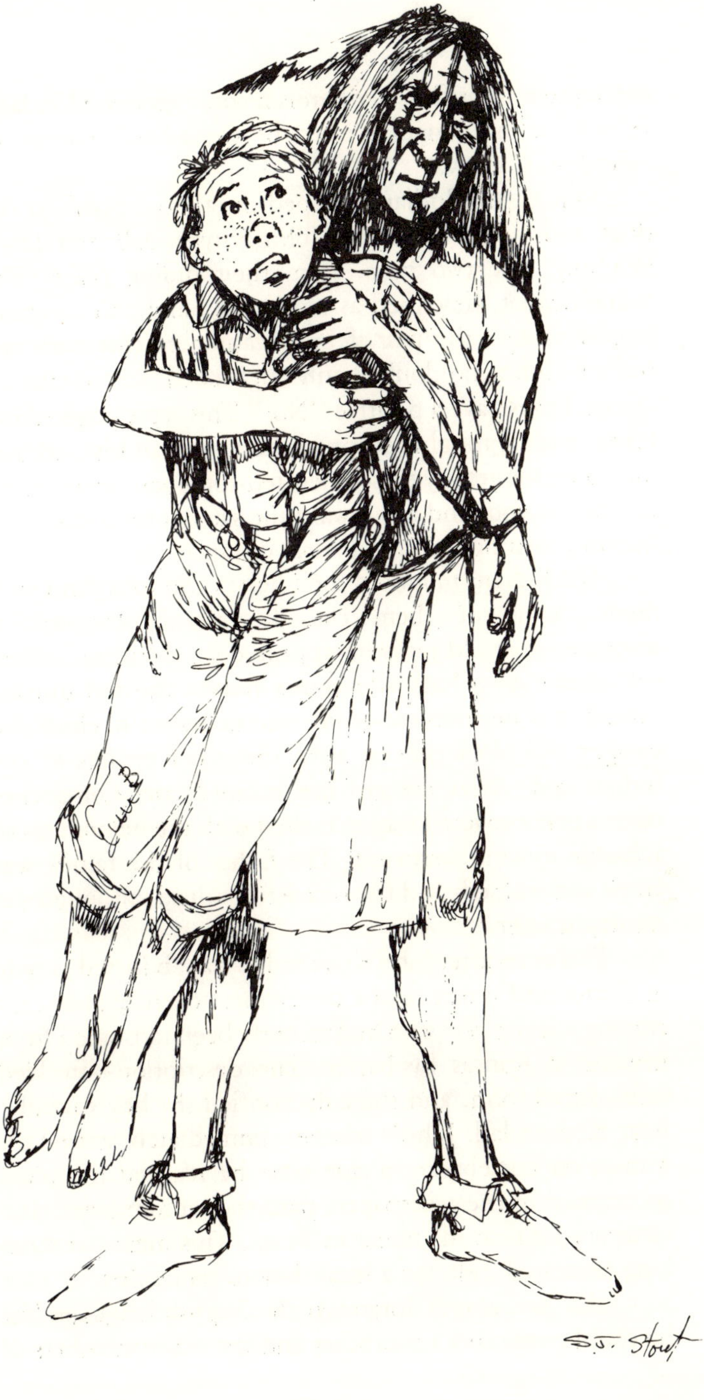
S.J. Stout

the supreme sacrifice, her heroism commemorated in later years by a monument erected by the school children of Hamilton County.

One of the Indians stepped on a loose plank in the floor and quickly dragged John Kuykendall and Lewis Manning, the two boys, from their hiding place. The Indian leader, described as red-headed and able to speak English, asked the pair if they wanted to ride with the Indians. John, no doubt badly frightened, stammered an assent. Lewis gave a positive "No!" This reply angered the leader and he roughly stripped the boy of all his clothing, including his greatly prized new red-top boots. Lewis dashed out the door and ran toward the safety of the river, one Indian pursuing him for a short distance.

The Indians mounted their horses and took John with them. Some of them chased Amanda Howard, a seventeen-year-old girl who appeared on the scene, riding side-saddle on a half-wild young horse. The girl quickly turned, put her horse to a run, and managed to elude the savages and then ride to warn the other settlers of the Indian raid. After the girl had escaped, the Comanches came upon a covered wagon loaded with the belongings of a family moving westward. The father of the family was killed and scalped, and the wife left for dead, although she recovered later.

Two years after John Kuykendall was abducted, a lady in Hamilton County read a newspaper advertisement concerning a white boy who had recently been ransomed from Indians in Kansas by barter. The description—freckled face—fitted John, and the lady notified the boy's family. Isaac Kuykendall, John's brother, immediately started for Kansas on horseback. In due time he reached the place mentioned in the newspaper, paid the ransom price, and returned John to his home in Texas. This meant another long horseback ride for a small boy to remember.

John had almost forgotten the English language but he could remember his brother and the other members of his family. Never forgotten by John, in the remaining years of a long life, was his long ride with the Indians, mounted bareback and feet tied under the horse, day and night until the Indians were safely out of the country.

AUTHOR'S NOTE: The monument honoring the heroism of the teacher, Miss Ann Whitney, stands in the courthouse yard at Hamilton, Texas. The funds to pay for the monument were raised by the school children of Hamilton, County.

## 17. Children Stolen By Indians In Austin

In 1842, only three years after Austin had been selected as the frontier capital "city" of the Republic of Texas, Emma and Thomas Simpson were kidnapped by Indians in daylight. Late one afternoon Mrs. Simpson sent her fourteen-year-old daughter and twelve-year-old son to drive in the milk cows, only a short distance from their home near present Congress Avenue. The mother heard the children screaming and then saw them being carried away by Indians. The mother's screams soon alarmed the village and a band of men started in pursuit. The trail led by way of Mount Bonnell and was difficult to follow due to the rough terrain. Darkness ended the chase and the red men escaped.

The grief stricken mother heard nothing of her children for more than a year. Finally, Thomas was ransomed from the Indians by a trader at Taos, New Mexico. He was finally returned home to his mother and the story of his experiences became known.

The boy told that his sister fought the Indians every foot of the way as the marauders fled from Austin. The Indians held and carried her by force and treated her roughly. Thomas was guarded by two warriors and realized that if he resisted he would be killed. He tried in vain to get his sister to submit peacefully. The Indians divided into two bands and when they reunited, on Shoal Creek about six miles from Austin, Thomas saw his sister's scalp hanging to the saddle of one of the Indians. Later the bones of the unfortunate girl were found and the boy's story corroborated.

Thomas was with the Indians for more than a year. His grueling horseback ride with the wandering savages was enough to satisfy any boy's craving for adventure and travel. He was delighted to get home!

## 18. Willie Lehmann Rode Six Days As An Indian Captive

One of the most vivid first-person accounts given by former Indian captives is the description of his six-day ride given by Willie Lehmann. Although the account was written some thirty years after his experience, Willie could recall every detail of his unforgettable ride.

Nine year-old Willie Lehmann, Herman his brother, and two small sisters were sent to the wheat field to scare away the birds one day in 1870. These children of German-American parentage were enjoying all the wonders of nature in their Loyal Valley, Mason County, Texas, home when Indians suddenly appeared. The children ran for the safety of their home but the two boys were captured. Willie was slung on a horse behind a warrior, while Herman was tied on a horse. The band rode east at a fast gallop, over hills and rocks. The forked-stick saddle in front of Willie gored him as they bounced along.

Finally, the Indians stopped on top of a high hill. Two Indians on foot went forward. Willie recalled that one of the redskins wore a bright silver breast plate on his chest and a funny cap with a big rooster's feather on his head. These Indians followed a trail until they were out of sight. Another savage climbed a tree and watched them with field glasses. After a time the pair returned with two horses—a sorrel, with a star in his forehead, and a gray.

While the Indians were holding a "palaver" a man, riding a gray horse and leading a dun, passed near by. The Indians scattered and tried to catch him but he rode around the point of a hill. The boys, with their guard watched and saw the man reappear at a distance. He dismounted from the gray and tried to bridle the dun but the animal seemed wild and put up quite a struggle. The man then remounted the gray and rode pell-mell over rocks and gullies. The Indians did not catch him.

One Indian held the boys on a high hill and they watched the Indians fighting in the valley below. The two boys tried to escape when they saw that their guard was intent on the scene below. The Indian caught them, mounted them as before, and the three rode to meet the others. The Indians had captured several horses from Stark Mosely. The band moved on, with Herman's horse running loose with the herd. Occasionally the animal would wander away from the other horses and Herman tried to get him to leave the band entirely. But Herman could not control the horse and before long they were right back with the Indians. After another fast ride, the Indians stopped long enough to try to put Willie on a wild horse but the horse was too tough for even these expert horsemen to handle. Whenever the savages came upon a hog or a yearling (cattle) they would give chase, a rider on either side, and use their lances until the animal fell. Willie saw the green grass turn red with blood along the trail. Once the savages found a very young calf and tortured it by sticking spears into its tender feet.

Willie was not tied at night when the Indians made camp but he had little chance to escape. Herman was tied fast and the Indians were always on guard. Willie's guard showed some kindnesses and never beat or abused him, although he scared the boy very much. He gave Willie a pair of moccasins and also a small peculiar fur cap, with ears standing straight up like a frightened jack rabbit. The burly Indian once took Willie's shirt, which had been restored to him, and tried to put it on but laughingly returned it when he found that it was far too small. Willie was often alone with his guard when the Indians separated to steal more horses. He saw this Indian kill several domestic animals and one panther. The savage ate some of the meat raw and offered some of it to the boy but never forced him to eat it.

Once the guard pointed toward his horse tied some distance away but Willie did not understand what he wanted. The Indian drew his gun and pointed it at the boy. Willie walked to the horse, then came back. The Indian growled and scolded angrily, rushed at the boy—and Willie thought his time had come. The savage rushed past Willie, untied his horse, mounted quickly, pulled the boy up behind him, and they rode on.

Both the Lehmann boys were painted by their captors to look like Indians but neither enjoyed their experiences at the time. They became tired, stiff, and sore all over. At one muddy pool of water, all the riders dismounted to drink. An Indian slipped up behind Willie and soused his head into the mud. Another did Herman the same. Then the Indians laughed loudly. To the boys the food was unspeakable. At first, when the Indians were in a great hurry to get out of the country, they ate raw liver and meat with the blood dripping from it. The boys could not endure the sight. Later, as the Indians traveled more leisurely, they took the time to cook the meat a little and the boys began to eat a little but without salt or bread it was not to their taste. The Indians were kind enough to grease the sores on the boys' bodies and this gave slight relief.

One of the Indian men had a crippled leg and riding on horseback hurt him. As the Indians began to travel along leisurely, this man began to walk much of the time. About the sixth day soldiers suddenly came upon them and stampeded the whole outfit. The crippled Indian tried to catch one of the loose horses but was unable to do so. Willie was riding a little brown pony at the time. The crippled Indian saw the boy, grabbed the pony, and jumped up in front of Willie. The other Indians had already left the scene in wild flight. The crippled redskin now goaded the pony to his top speed but they fell farther and farther behind their companions. The Indian tried to crowd Willie off the horse, thus to lighten the burden. Willie held to the Indian for dear life. But the Indian kept edging back on the pony, pushing Willie a little at a time, and finally Willie had nothing left to sit upon or hold. He fell in a bed of rocks but was not seriously injured. He saw no soldiers come near and after a time he started to walk through the chaparral bushes.

The starving nine year-old boy was far from the nearest white settlement. Lost and famished, weary and homesick—but he did not give up. He found water and followed a ravine. He expected some wild animal to attack him at any time. Big buck deer came right up to him, no doubt curious to see the unusual sight of human being on foot. Also, Willie thought that his peculiar cap with the funny ears attracted the interest of the bucks. When night came on, he was so exhausted that he fell asleep at once. Finally he came to a stage road and found a piece of corn bread, which some freighter had probably tossed aside. He blew away some of the dirt and devoured it. He waited in the road and at length a man came along, but since he spoke English and Willie spoke German they could not converse. The man moved on and Willie blamed his cap and the fact that he was still painted like an Indian for not being rescued. Soon afterward another man in a wagon came along. The man spoke to Willie in German and told him not to hide or be scared. The man hugged the boy and both of them cried. Willie told his story. The man gave Willie food and took him to the nearest settlement and left him with a family until he delivered his load of freight. In due time the man took Willie back to his family in Loyal Valley. He would take no pay but Willie gave him his one moccasin. The cap had been left in the bushes along the road. The reunion with his family was also something that Willie never forgot.

AUTHOR'S NOTE: Jonathan H. Jones, in his book *Indianology*, published in 1899, wrote the first-person account of Willie Lehmann's had tried to loose the rawhide thongs binding his wrists but about all he did was rub the skin off his arms.

A husky Indian placed Pete on a horse and mounted behind him. The raiders started their fast ride to get away from the scene of the murder. The rawhide cut deeper and deeper into Pete's arms and legs. The jolting of the horse was torture to the boy but there was no stop for rest until late that night. When a stop was made, the boy was too weary and sleepy to eat. After a few hours of sleep, he was suffering so greatly that he had to bite back the pain. Early the next morning, the ride was continued, with scouts on all sides to see if there was any pursuit. After a few days, the pace slackened and the Indians rested and began to hunt.

One morning an Indian scout returned to camp and, after an exciting pow-wow, they ran to their horses and rode away in a hurry. The next few days were a nightmare to Pete. The Indians did not beat him but they did keep him bound tightly. They traveled at night only and hid during the day. Their only food was small game such as birds, rabbits, and squirrels which could be killed with bows and arrows. The meat was kept and eaten even after it was spoiled. Pete was nauseated by the stench and, although he had never even tasted tobacco, he began to crave a chew of tobacco. He imagined that a chew would relieve his hunger pains. His body became thin and scrawny. At night the homesick, starving boy cried himself to sleep. This went on for three long weeks but Pete had lost count of time and was desperately trying to stay alive. He noted that the Indians showed fear that they were being followed.

One morning as Pete lay bound and feeling more dead than alive, an Indian scout returned to camp and usual council was held. This ended by an Indian cutting the bonds that had held Pete's hands and feet for more than three weeks and then all the Indians jumped on their horses and rode away.

Pete could not stand on his numb feet, nor could he call out to the white men who rode near him. Painfully he began trying to walk but all that he could do at first was stagger a few feet before he fell. He found a few berries to eat. But almost miraculously some cowboys from a nearby ranch found the boy and tenderly carried him to the ranch house. He shook his head when asked if he was hungry. Instead, he asked for a chew of tobacco. Ill and emaciated, Pete was nursed back to health and restored to his mother, who had given him up for dead.

## 20. Tehan, The Red Headed Kiowa Warrior

Tehan received his name because he was captured by the Kiowa Indians in Texas when he was a very small boy. The name was variously spelled—Tahan, Texan, or Tejano. By the time he was eighteen, he was a giant of a fellow and was quite an oddity among the Indians due to the fact that he had fiery red hair. He had already been on a raid with chief Big Bow deep into Texas and was thus a recognized warrior.

In 1874, the Kiowas and Comanches fled from their reservation at Fort Sill and headed back for the Staked Plains. Tehan, along the trail, turned back to look for some horses that had strayed from their previous camp. The other Indians tried to prevent him from going, pointing out that the soldiers were all over the country. Laughing scornfully, Tehan replied, "I am a white man. I can understand their language. I am not afraid."

A detachment of troops caught up with Tehan a few hours later. He was riding a dun mule and all of his attention was apparently centered on following the trail of a wounded deer. The soldiers saw that he was white and when they found that he lived with the Indians, offered to send him back to his own people. Tehan made it appear that he was delighted with the offer and rode all day with the soldiers. He was then turned over to the captain of a wagon train which was hauling supplies to the troops. The Indians attacked this train and held them in camp by a long-range siege. By that time Tehan had convinced the whites that he was one of them. When a party of "walk-soldiers" made a dash to the waterhole, Tehan was right with them—but he did not return to the wagons. Instead, he hurried to the Indian camp and was joyfully received. He was wearing a new army uniform, the envy of every Indian. The Indians asked Tehan why he had left his own people and come back to them. To this he replied that he liked to eat raw liver so well that he was going to stay an Indian. Many cases are on record of white boys thus becoming totally Indianized.

When practically all the Kiowas and Comanches had been placed on the reservation, Tehan joined Big Bow, an arrogant chief, who held out to the last. Big Bow led his band to the West and continued to raid in the vast unoccupied range. At last the cavalry was sent in to run them down. The crafty Big Bow had committed so many depredations and crimes that he was afraid to surrender, as most of the other chiefs had done. He reasoned that Tehan, who was white, would be induced to tell all that he knew and thus it would not do to let Tehan be taken prisoner by the whites. Soon afterward, Tehan met his death in a very mysterious manner. Big Bow went into the agency and surrendered but was never imprisoned or punished.

## 21. Pedro Espinosa, Boy Captive Of The Comanches

Pedro Espinosa was born on a ranch on the Rio Grande, near Laredo. At the age of nine he was made captive by a raiding band of Comanches, who cruelly murdered the adult inhabitants of the area and carried the children into captivity. At first he was treated just as the

Comanches treated their own children but watched all the time. As usual with Indian boys, he was made to herd the horses. At the age of thirteen, Pedro accompanied the Comanches on a raid against the Tonkawas. His job was to take care of the horses but he managed to show so much grit and nerve that the Comanches made him a warrior.

To all outward appearances, Pedro became completely Indianized. He bartered for more than one wife. He fought alongside the braves of the tribe and he became a crafty horse thief. He participated in cruel outrages with the marauders. In spite of all this Pedro was never permitted to go near the Rio Grande, although parties of warriors were always making excursions into Mexico. Perhaps the suspicious Comanches understood his real feelings; for he never forgot his native land, the atrocious murder of his family, and actually held a deep, silent, and bitter hatred for the savages.

Pedro related that once while the Comanches were encamped on Brady's Creek, now in McCulloch County, Texas, he carefully observed the preparations made by a party of youths, none over the age of nineteen, for a raid into Mexico as far as Monterrey. None of the boys had ever been in Mexico before. The elders of the tribe gathered the young men, seated them in a circle, and instructed them as to the country to be covered. One old man drew a map on the ground and indicated every prominent landmark for each day of the journey. The Indians were so skilled in plains-craft that they could remember every detail of the country. In this manner, Pedro also became possessed of uncanny skill in following a trail.

After living with the Comanches for nineteen years, Pedro was permitted to go on a bear hunt, his skill as a hunter being well established. One night while his companions slept, he crawled from the camp, took two horses and managed to escape. After a long, hard ride he reached the site of his old home near Laredo. Here he settled down among his relatives, married in due time, and became a respected member of the community. But nothing in that section was safe from the Comanches and after a time he offered his services to the United States army as a guide, scout and trailer.

Lieutenant Richard I. Dodge, who was stationed at Fort Lincoln, Texas, in 1849, highly commended Pedro. The boy who had been brought up as a thief was honest and faithful to every trust. His ability as a trailer was little short of a marvel. He led the troops for hundreds of miles on the trail of the red marauders. For many years Pedro faithfully served the government. In 1861, during the intense excitement of the secession of Texas from the Union, General Twiggs sent Pedro with a message to some of the Union troops who had left San Antonio, expecting to leave the State by way of the coast. Pedro Espinosa was captured by some of the secessionists, who after reading the dispatches, shot Pedro to death.

## 22. Temple Friend Was "Indianized" After Years With The Comanches

The story of Lee Temple Friend has received considerable attention in federal and state archives, in contemporary newspapers, and in stories concerning the early Southwest.

In February of 1868, a band of nineteen mounted Comanche braves, accompanied by three squaws, surrounded the cabin of John Friend in Legion Valley, about sixteen miles from Llano, Texas. Eight women and children were staying at the home, with no man near enough for protection. Their names were: Matilda Friend, whose father had been killed and scalped by Indians a few years previously; her step-son, eight-year-old Lee Temple Friend; Mrs. Boy Johnson and her infant; Mrs. Babe Johnson and infant; Amanda Townsend, eighteen and unmarried; and eleven-year-old Melinda Cordle (or Caudle).

Matilda Friend, with a whispered prayer, took her husband's big Springfield rifle and prepared to fight the howling fiends to the last. She placed the gun across the ironing board, aimed at the door now being battered by the savages. She heard a ripping sound at the opposite end of the cabin and was horrified to see a painted Indian rip one of the pickets from the wall. She swung the heavy rifle muzzle to bear on the new threat. Just then the bar holding the door cracked like a pistol shot and a giant brave sprang inside the small room. The brave woman swung the long rifle back to shoot the fiend. The brave jumped, seized the gun, and wrenched it from her grasp. The Comanche at the hole in the wall fired an arrow, striking Mrs. Friend in the left arm, the bloody head going through. The big brave tried to shoot her with the gun but she knocked the weapon aside with a chair. The big Indian rushed at his victim but she grabbed a large smoothing iron, smashed it against the man's head, and knocked him down. Another arrow caught her in the side, then a third struck full in the breast. The plucky woman fell and perhaps fainted but when the murderer slashed her scalp she seized the knife blade and was badly cut across the hand. The savage then slugged her several times with the knife handle and left her for dead. Somehow, she recovered enough to watch the savages seize all the others in the house and drag them outside to waiting horses. One of the wretches, making a last trip into the house, gave the arrow piercing the woman's breast several sharp jerks. It would not pull free. Mrs. Friend steeled herself not to flinch or in any manner visibly respond regardless of the agony suffered. The savage grunted several times and then ran from the cabin. The heroic woman, in intense pain and very near death, staggered and crawled a distance of a mile and one-half through the snow to the house of a neighbor. The news of the tragedy was spread and a posse took up the Indian trail the next morning.

The mutilated bodies of the three women and the two

babies were found within a few miles of the Friend home. The Indian trail was lost in the rocky mountainous area. Lee Temple Friend and Malinda Cordle were not found and it was supposed that the Indians had taken them out of the country.

*The Austin Daily Republican* of June 1, 1868, and in the weeks following, carried an appeal by John S. Friend, the father of the boy, asking all agents and traders in the Indian country to look out for the two children. On July 18, 1868, Texas Governor E. M. Pease issued a letter of credit to Leonard S. Friend, grandfather of the boy, for the sum of $1,500 and appointed him agent of the State of Texas to secure the release of the two children and other captives from Texas "held as Prisoners of War by the Indians." It was supposed that the guilty Indians were somewhere near Council Grove, Kansas.

No description is available of the excruciating

horseback ride of the two children from Llano County, Texas, to Kansas. It is safe to conclude that it was no pleasure trip. Melinda Cordle was restored to her family after some eight months of existence with the Comanches. In due time the plucky girl wrote to John Friend, the father, who had then moved to Kansas, informing him that Temple was still alive. With rekindled hope the boy's father and grandfather continued their search through the vast Indian country. Their efforts were still unsuccessful and in the meantime Temple was becoming completely "Indianized."

Three weeks after the Indians had removed a small portion of the scalp of Matilda Friend and left her for dead, the pioneer mother gave birth to a healthy baby girl. As soon as possible, John Friend moved his family back to El Dorado, Kansas, where Reverend Leonard S. Friend was minister of the Methodist Church. John Friend settled down to farming—and searching for his son when his other duties permitted. The grandfather devoted his life to the search, traveling some fifteen thousand miles and as far as the Apache reservations in Arizona and New Mexico. The elderly preacher, traveling alone in a buggy, preached here and there at far-flung Indian agencies, frontier military posts and villages. He frequently visited the Kiowa-Comanche agency at Fort Sill, Indian Territory.

In 1873, Reverend Friend received a letter from Laurie Tatum, Quaker agent at the Fort Sill reservation, stating that two white boys had been recovered from the Indians. One of them could be Temple Friend. Horseback, a friendly Comanche chief, had brought the boys to Tatum. The grandfather immediately started for Fort Sill in his buggy. Agent Tatum, in his book *Our Red Brothers*, described the touching scene of the meeting of the old grandfather and the grandson. The boy did not seem to recognize his relative at first. When first brought to the agency, Temple could speak Comanche only but not one word of English. After spending some time in the agency school, he began to understand some English words. The old gentleman lovingly embraced the youth and said, "Temple Friend." The boy looked at him in wonder, then answered "Yes." The old man and the boy were soon traveling northward toward the Friend home in Kansas. Reverend Friend had kept posted a standing reward of one thousand dollars for the recovery of Temple but, thanks to friendly Chief Horseback and Agent Tatum, the boy was secured free of cost.

Lee Temple Friend, now thirteen, had become a Comanche in the past five years. Almost constantly on the back of a fast horse, he had learned to love the wild, roving life. To all observers he was all Indian. He had forgotten the white man's language and manner of living. The father and grandfather worked patiently with the boy but he showed little response and learned only a few words of English. Curious white neighbors frightened him. The hum-drum life on a farm and living inside a house depressed him and the white man's food was unbearable and not digestible. In spirit and body, the lad wasted away, longing all the time for life on the open range. Within a few months Temple Friend was dead.

Matilda Friend, the heroic pioneer mother, gradually recovered from her ordeal and years of travail in Texas. She had five more daughters. The dollar-sized scalp wound never healed and until her death, in 1909, had to be dressed daily. John Friend continued to live in Kansas, reaching the age of almost one-hundred. He always sorrowed for his lost son.

## 23. The Jackson Children Rode Eight Days With Indian Horse Thieves

John Williams, Texas Ranger Captain, in October of 1858, tersely reported for future archives that he and his men followed an Indian trail and came to the home of Joshua Jackson, then located in Brown County, Texas. The house was deserted. Two miles further the Rangers came upon a grim and tragic scene. (The accounts vary greatly as to the details, even to Jackson's Christian name.)

The father, mother, a seventeen-year-old daughter, and one small child had been brutally murdered. The body of the teenage girl was badly mutilated and her throat had been cut. Two young sons, according to Ranger Williams, escaped from the Indians and told the Rangers that two other members of the family—a girl of about nine and a boy about twelve—had been carried off by the savages. The Rangers buried the bodies of the murdered settlers where they had fallen, then spread the alarm, and took up the trail of the Indians. When the news of the Jackson family tragedy was spread along the frontier, there was intense excitement over a large area.

The Indians continued their marauding raids; stealing horses to add to an ever increasing herd, pillaging, and murdering or kidnapping any unwary victims. They moved eastward into Coryell County, at least a hundred miles from the Jackson home. Rangers and settlers followed hot on the trail, made difficult to follow because the Indians frequently split into small bands only to unite later at a designated landmark.

Ranger Lieutenant D. C. Cowan reported several days later that the two Jackson children had been recovered, having been abandoned by their captors when the chase became too hot. One Ranger, riding at top speed, thought that he saw a human face in some bushes. Fearing that it was Indians no doubt, he summoned his companions and the thicket was surrounded. The children when discovered were afraid to call out, thinking that the Indians had returned. They were in a terrible condition. They had not eaten for eight days and were famished. The little girl especially had suffered agonies, not being accustomed to horseback riding. The boy had withstood his ordeal much better.

The Indians had forced the children to ride bareback

on ponies without bridles and herded along with the loose horses. These animals were driven at a fast gait, sometimes through dense brush. The young riders were practically disrobed and were scratched from head to foot. The exhausted children were taken in charge by families living at Camp Colorado, in Coleman County, and finally restored to relatives at Lampasas. Rebecca Jackson, with the passing of time, recovered from her harrowing ordeal but could never forget the tragic experiences following the massacre of her family. Her brother, Joshua, Jr., was not so fortunate. The inhuman atrocities which he had lived through left him broken and mentally deranged. Jackson descendants still live in the area.

## 24. Williams Girl Stolen In Brown County

    The hard-riding red raiders once again showed their brutal savagery when they surrounded the Bill Williams home on Sand Creek, in Brown County, Texas late in 1873. Early one morning, the pioneer mother was inside a rail pen milking her cows, with her baby sitting nearby. The father and son were cutting rails some distance away. The twelve-year-old daughter was working inside the log cabin. Suddenly the Indians showered the body of Mrs. Williams with arrows, then fiendishly dragged the baby through a fire until it was badly burned. The young daughter was carried away by the savages, who eluded their pursuers and got out of the country.
    The numerous accounts of the captivity and fate of the Williams girl vary greatly as to details. Some time later, the body of a young American girl was found by a surveying crew on the Salt Fork of the Brazos, some two hundred miles from the Williams home. This was identified as the Williams girl. One account states that the body found by the surveyors was hanging to the limb of a tree, suspended by a split girth of a saddle. The girth was said to have

belonged to a side-saddle owned by Mrs. Williams. Evidence showed that the red fiends had scalped the child alive. It was believed that the savages had killed her when she became so exhausted that she could not ride one mile farther. The surveyors buried the body in an unmarked grave, one of the countless such graves in the vast unsettled West.

Bill Williams, the father, made every effort possible to locate his daughter. When he learned her fate, he became maddened by sorrow and grief, already unbearable due to the murder of his wife and baby. He became an Indian hater, joined the Texas Rangers, and became known as "Wild Bill Williams."

## 25. Riggs Girls Had Brief But Memorable Captivity

A tombstone in the cemetery at Killeen, Texas, bears this epitaph: "John and Jane Riggs, murdered by Comanche Indians, March 16, 1859." This headstone had originally been placed at the graves of the couple in the Sugar Loaf Cemetery but was moved to Killeen when the old grave yard was taken into the Fort Hood reservation. Today it is a reminder of the dangers of frontier life.

In March of 1859, Indians made a daylight horse-stealing raid into western Bell County, murdering and kidnapping any unwary whites in their path. A few families had settled near Sugar Loaf Mountain, near Cow House Creek and west of Belton, now enclosed by the far-flung Fort Hood military reservation. The Riggs family had only recently moved into the area and started building their home. They were unaccustomed to life on the Indian frontier. John Riggs, the father, along with his neighbor named Pierce and sixteen-year-old David Elms, was out early one morning hauling cedar rails. Pierce and young Elms, in a wagon some distance in advance of Riggs, were ambushed by Indians. Pierce was killed at once. Dave Elms ran to save his life but was run down by the mounted redskins, who immediately stripped the boy of all his clothing. When he resisted, the savages whipped him unmercifully.

Riggs saw the attack on his companions, abandoned his wagon and team, ran the short distance to his house, and started with his family to the house of a neighbor. The Indians saw them in the open, left one brave to guard their boy prisoner, and quickly raced toward the unprotected Riggs family.

Two small boys hid in the grass and escaped. Both parents were killed and scalped. Somehow, the baby of the family was left unhurt. Two small girls were grabbed by the brawny savages, each mounted behind an Indian.

The Indian guarding Dave Elms became so engrossed in the slaughtering of the Riggs parents that the boy was able to slip away and hide. All the Indians were so eager to plunder the Riggs home that they made little effort to hunt the boy. Dave started toward the nearest house but soon met a Mr. Lee, who on horseback hastened to spread the alarm. Within a short time a posse of seasoned Indian fighters met at the scene of the murder. The Riggs baby was found unhurt crawling around on the ground covered with the blood of the father and mother. The settlers were soon following the trail of the large horse herd driven by the red men.

After plundering the Riggs home, the Indians rode southward for several miles at a run, then turned west. The captive girls were held tightly by their captors in the mad race. The going was rough, up hill and down hill, through bushes and thickets. The girls were thankful for one rest period but the horror of what they saw overrode any personal sufferings. The Indians stopped their horses when they saw a man on horseback some few hundred yards away. The girls were forced to watch four of the red riders slip toward their victim, murder and scalp him after a brief chase. One more horse was added to the herd and one more scalp was tied to the saddle of a brave. In leaving the scene, the girls could hear the groans of the dying man.

The cavalcade was again put into rapid motion with loud whoops and yells. An Indian lookout on a high ridge gave warning that a band of horsemen was coming rapidly from the north. The Indians turned down a rough canyon, hazing the loose horses before them and applying their lariats to any animal which held them back. The pace became a mad race. The smaller of the Riggs girls fell from the horse upon which she had been held, back of an Indian rider, who apparently became so intent on flight that he released his hold. The older girl saw her sister fall. She realized that the savages were not going to stop for anything. She feared that her sister was badly injured by the fall. In desperation, she quickly jumped from the running horse. The Indian behind whom she rode felt her move, grabbed the girl's dress in one hand, and rode some distance with the helpless captive dangling by the horse's side. Her head and arms almost dragged the ground and bushes and thorns lacerated her flesh. Finally, she grasped a bush with one hand and held on like a bull dog. Her dress was torn from her body and the yelling savage horseman rode away, waving the garment in the air. The plucky girl lay bruised and bleeding. The Indians had no time to return for the captives and after a few moments the girl regained her feet and ran to her little sister.

The two girls now began a painful and weary walk on their back trail. They came to a deserted log cabin and spent the night there, suffering from cold and hunger. The next morning, the exhausted pair continued walking. They were utterly exhausted when they came to another deserted cabin. A man on horseback found them here, placed them upon his horse, and took them to the Dameron home. The girls were tenderly cared for and finally reunited with relatives.

The Indians were never overtaken but were forced to abandon many of their stolen horses. Dave Elms, whose brief span as an Indian captive was much too long, according to his own opinion, was ever afterward known as "Indian Dave Elms." He died many years later in Edwards County, Texas.

## 26. Adolph Kohn, Captured While Herding Sheep

The other white boy brought in with Temple Friend to agent Laurie Tatum at Fort Sill by Comanche Chief Horseback, was identified as Adolph Kohn (or Korn). This eleven-year-old German boy was captured by Arizona Apaches in Mason County, Texas, while herding sheep near his home. This was in 1870. The lad made the long, harrowing horseback ride westward with his captors. Surviving this ordeal, he was traded to the Quahada Comanches, one of the last of the nomadic Indian bands to hold out against and vainly resist the white men on the Staked Plains.

About three years after being captured, Adolph Kohn, along with Temple Friend, was taken to the Fort Sill agency. He told agent Tatum that he was eleven years of age, had a father, mother, and nine brothers and sisters. Tatum stated that the boy was delighted with the promise of being restored to his family.

J. Marvin Hunter, versatile Texas historian and former resident of Mason County, Texas, recorded that Adolph never did take to the Indian life, as did so many young boys. After he was restored to his family in Texas, he became a useful and respected citizen of Mason County.

## 27. Martha Virginia Webster Wrote Of Her Tribulations As An Indian Captive

John Webster, former Virginia Plantation owner, in 1839, moved westward—"lock, stock, and barrel"—intending to settle in present Burnet County, Texas. His family accompanied him—his wife, a son about eleven years of age, and Martha, the three-year-old daughter. Several wagons, each drawn by four yokes of oxen, were heavily laden with household goods and supplies. A herd of 300 head of cattle was driven along to establish the ranch. Twelve armed men were in the party, and also one negro servant. Webster planned to build a fort upon the land which he had previously surveyed.

When the caravan was some six miles from the destination, a very large band of mounted Indians appeared and threatened to attack them. The herd of cattle had already been stampeded and several of the men were riding to round up the strayed animals. Webster turned his wagons, back-tracked all night, and the party reached Brushy Creek, in Williamson County, about daybreak. Here, some 300 Indians attacked fiercely. The fighting continued until the last white man fell. Other warriors had joined in the fight to swell the Indian ranks to nearly a thousand.

Then followed an orgy of destructive vandalism. The savages broke or burned everything they could not carry away on their horses. The dead men were scalped and stripped of their clothing.

Mrs. Webster and her two children, after suffering through the fight, were forced to watch the savage orgy of destruction and mutilation and then placed on horses. The Indians started for their main encampment, never stopping until this was reached. The mother suffered agonies in mind and body. The son fought the Indians at every turn, much to their delight. Martha cried constantly. In the Indian camp, Mrs. Webster was forced to dress in Indian squaw garb, the son like the Indian boys, but Martha was deprived of all clothing during her entire captivity.

In 1912, Martha wrote: . . ."I don't know how I lived, the way the Indians tortured me. The devils burned and whipped me, and would often tie a rope around me and throw me into the river because I cried. I have scars on my body this day from burns. When we reached San Antonio (nearly a year after being captured) I had sores all over my body and it was winter too. Just think of me, being naked and one solid sore. And that is not all—they tied me on wild horses and turned them loose, and a lot of Indians would take after the horse, just to see me tortured . . ."

The son's fighting spirit gained the admiration of the Indians and he was soon accepted. Not so with the mother and daughter. The three members of the family were separated, each taken by a roving band, only to meet again at intervals. Such meeting places were Enchanted Rock, Santa Fe in New Mexico, and finally at the Devil's River, in Texas.

It was at this last rendezvous, on Devil's River, that the frantic mother made her third attempt to escape from her savage captors. She stole her suffering daughter, now nearing four, and slipped from the Comanche encampment. The mother was driven to desperation after seeing six young white girls killed by the red fiends. The mother had to carry the maimed daughter much of the time, so badly had the child's feet been burned by the Indian torturers. The mother had stolen a little dried meat but this did not last long. They traveled at night, kept away from the regular trails and watering places, and hid during the day. It took them twelve days and nights to cover the 300 miles to San Antonio and safety. Both were starved and utterly exhausted. The mother's feet were worn to the bone and bled at every step. The child could not walk alone and did not have one bit of clothing.

About that time the Republic of Texas was making a treaty with the Comanches and captives were to be exchanged. Six days after the Webster mother and daughter reached San Antonio, the son was brought in by the Comanches and surrendered. But the happy family reunion did not last long. The mother was never able to recover from her terrible ordeal. The two children were taken into the home of relatives. The son enlisted in the war with Mexico, in 1846, and died at Monterrey. Thus Martha Webster was an orphan at an early age.

At the age of seventeen, Martha Webster married and for a time lived in Burnet County on the land upon which her father had planned to settle. Later Martha and her husband lived in Lampasas and Gillespie Counties. Martha later remarried and moved to Oregon, then to California. The pioneer settlement of Strickling in Burnet County took its name for Martha's first husband, M. D. Strickling.

In 1936, Texas Centennial year, the graves of the victims of the Comanche massacre, were located near Leander, Williamson County, and commemorative markers placed upon the site.

In 1912, Martha Virginia Webster Simmons, and her children, were living in California. At that time, nearly three-quarters of a century since her captivity, she wrote her story of horror. Young as she was at the time of the tragedy, much of the story was indelibly impressed upon her mind. Some of the story, of course, was later told to her by relatives. Such were the vicissitudes of life on the Indian frontier in days gone by.

NOTE: Information concerning Martha Webster's story is from *Frontier Times,* Vol. 14, No. 9, June 1937, published at Bandera, Texas, by the late J. Marvin Hunter. This was copied from *The Burnet Bulletin,* no date given.

## 28. Indians Took The German Sisters From Kansas To Texas

Unfortunate whites who were taken captives by Indians were usually taken to distant places away from their homes. Those from Texas might make the long horseback ride to Kansas, Indian Territory, New Mexico, or Mexico. The story of the German (or Germaine) sisters is somewhat different. They were taken captive in Kansas and made the long horseback journey to the Staked Plains of Texas and then finally returned to Kansas.

In September of 1870, John German, his wife Lydia, and seven children were traveling across the plains of Kansas in a covered wagon, searching for a homestead in the West. Early one morning seventeen painted Cheyenne horsemen and two squaws suddenly raced down a hill and surrounded the wagon. There followed one of the bloodiest massacres perpetrated in the West. The father and mother were killed before they could defend themselves. Three of the older children were brutally murdered. The four daughters left alive were forced to witness the horrors of murder and scalping of their loved ones. The wagon and its contents were burned and the cattle killed for meat.

Two of the girls, Addie and Julie, ages seven and five, were placed on a horse and put in charge of one of the squaws, who had been able to keep a brute of a savage from killing them on the spot. Seventeen-year-old Katherine and twelve-year-old Sophia were mounted on separate horses, each behind a mounted Indian. The flight to the Indian camp was a nightmare for the girls. In order to get away from the scene of the murder, the Indians rode fast—up hill, down hill, across streams and gullies. The girls became so weary that they were bound to their horses. There was no stopping for rest. Hour after hour, the band rode without food or water. Upon reaching the Indian camp, the lot of the girls was not improved. Cruel squaws beat them and Indian children tormented them. The food offered to them was half cooked meat, with blood dripping from it. The terrified sisters were forced to watch the Cheyennes celebrate the massacre with a scalp dance and they were constantly reminded of their murdered family by seeing the scalps flaunted on shields and lances.

Kicking Horse, leader of this band of Cheyennes, led the way to the Arkansas River, attacked the stockade at Pierceville, then fled southward across the Canadian River into rough country.

The two younger sisters were protected, fed, and cared for by a guardian squaw but the two older girls were made to suffer. All the squaws, except the one kind guardian, showed hatred for the white girls and tried to make life as miserable for them as possible.

The eldest sister, Katherine, tried to set a pattern for her sisters. She laughed at the squaws and refused to be frightened by the men. When the latter threatened to throw her into the Canadian to drown, she laughingly dived into the water, quickly swam across and on the return put on an exhibition of diving. The braves showed respect after this incident.

Late in September, the horseback nomads reached McClellan Creek, in the Texas Panhandle, some 230 miles from the unhappy massacre site. As the Indians began to make camp, the chief saw signs that United States troops had camped there recently. He quickly led his band on another flight deep into the Staked Plains, the last refuge of the Plains Indians.

The two small sisters were tied to the back of horses and as they bounced about on the galloping ponies, their bodies absorbed a terrible punishment. Both began to cry. The chief ordered them taken some distance from the band and killed. They could not be permitted to give warning to the soldiers, nor hold up the flight of the Indians. The protective squaw and her husband led away the ponies upon which the girls were mounted. The two older sisters were forced to observe this and then note the return of the squaw and her warrior, without the young girls.

But the kind squaw had obstinately defied the chief's order, overridden her man's objections, and saw the two children left alone in a vast forbidding wilderness far from any white settlement. Ultimate death was almost certain for the girls, but thanks to the squaw they had some chance for survival. The little girls began to walk aimlessly. Fortunately they came to a stream and their thirst was quenched. They had nothing to eat. One old shawl and a piece of ragged blanket was the only covering for their half-naked bodies. The cool night air made them shiver and they hugged each other for some warmth. Wolves gathered around but the girls did not realize their danger. They were so weary that sleep came quickly. Weak with hunger and fatigue, the sisters started walking the next morning. On a creek bank they found an old campsite of soldiers and there picked up a few scraps of meat and hardtack. They ate ravenously, walked on, and later found some berries and wild grapes.

The two small girls saw the passage of one day after another as they trudged on—in a circle. They came to two more old camps and picked up more hardtack. Their big prize was an old castaway horse-blanket, which kept them warm at night.

In the meantime, the soldiers found the bodies of the murdered Germans at the scene of the massacre in Kansas and from the list of names in the family Bible surmised that the four German girls had been carried into captivity. General Nelson Miles, with the Sixth Cavalry, was ordered to follow the Cheyennes and recover the girls.

The two youngest German waifs, wandered over the wild, uninhabited Staked Plains. Their bodies became emaciated and their scant clothing was in rags. One day a band of mounted Indians surrounded the girls, who were too exhausted to walk any farther. The savages jabbered excitedly, then picked up the children and took them to the main Cheyenne camp, in which the two older sisters were also captives. It was dark when the young girls were brought into camp, so the other sisters did not know of their presence. The squaws fed roasted buffalo meat to the starving girls and they fell into a sound sleep. They were awakened at dawn by a mad confusion of barking dogs, screaming squaws, and gunfire. A detachment of General Miles troops had attacked the Cheyenne camp, but the surprise was not complete. Fighting continued back and forth through the camp for hours, ending when the Indians fled and left their camp and all supplies in the hands of the soldiers.

The soldiers discovered the two young German sisters. Both were mere skeletons and almost naked. During the fight, some of the soldiers noted that Cheyenne braves were firing arrows into a buffalo robe lying near the edge of the village. The troopers soon found a small, unkempt white girl under the robe. The other sister was found in a lodge trying to build a fire. The frightened girls were overjoyed at the sight of the soldiers. Dr. J. L. Powell, who was with the troops, took the girls in his ambulance to Camp Supply. The officer's wives took the girls in charge, fed and clothed them, and gave them motherly care and comfort. Later the girls were taken to Fort Dodge and then to Fort Leavenworth, where they were placed in the care of the Patrick Corney family.

When Katherine and Sophia, the two older sisters,

were taken to the main Cheyenne camp on the Plains of Texas, their reception was far from pleasant. Their captors put on their war paint, mounted their best horses, tied the five fresh scalps to their rifles, and made triumphant entry into the main camp, yelling and firing their guns. Those in the camp rushed out to greet the returning band. The white girls were thrown from their ponies in the mad confusion. They began to run in order to avoid the stampede but the shrieking Cheyennes ran after the girls and tore their clothes to shreds. Each girl was then taken as a slave by a husky squaw, who warded off the others. A giant celebration kept the girls from sleeping that night.

Katherine and Sophia were made to carry wood and water and perform other menial camp tasks. The squaw who owned Katherine beat the girl unmercifully the first day. Sophia's squaw punished her victim with vicious slaps. The girls tried to make the best of their lot and the squaws in time showed some kindness. The girls were clothed, furnished with moccasins, and ate when the Indians had food.

The Cheyennes on the Plains at this time were in trouble. They were often hungry and continually on the move, in order to avoid the soldiers. The Cheyennes split into two bands and the sisters were separated. One band went to a tributary of the Pecos River in New Mexico, while the other went to the Rio Grande. General Miles, hearing that the Indians were near starvation, sent a Kiowa messenger to the chief, carrying a photograph of the two younger German sisters. Across the back of this Miles wrote a note to Katherine and Sophia saying that the two little sisters were well and in good hands. The older girls were not to be discouraged. The Kiowa was instructed to tell the Cheyenne chief that he was being held personally responsible for the safety and welfare of the captive whites and if the Cheyennes would come in immediately and surrender they would be fed and clothed. Chief Stone Calf, by slow stages and in severe winter weather, led his starving people to the Cheyenne agency at Fort Reno, Indian Territory. The sisters were sent to the Mission school at Darlington. The Cheyennes gave the girls presents and their squaw "owners" openly showed their grief in parting. In September of 1875, the two girls were sent to Fort Leavenworth and General Miles was appointed their guardian. Congress granted the sum of $12,500 to the four German sisters and all were educated. All four of them married and reared families. The story of their long ride and the horrors of their captivity with the Cheyennes became classic in the West.

## 29. The Mystery of Johnnie Ledbetter

During the Civil War, W. H. Ledbetter pre-empted land which contained known salt deposits located on the Salt Fork of Hubbard Creek, in Shackelford County, Texas. He erected a house and began to boil the water in order to obtain salt for sale. In time, he erected three block houses and brought his family to live on this extreme frontier outpost. Usually he had a few men employed to assist with the salt making and as protection against the Indians.

The Comanches were not long in showing their resentment to Ledbetter's encroachment upon their territory. They attacked his house and for years kept up their warfare against Ledbetter. After the Civil War several ranchmen brought their families into the area and the Ledbetters, like most of those families who became accustomed to Indian raids, were lulled into a sense of false security. They simply became careless in their disregard to the red menace.

J. C. Lynch, a neighboring ranchman, started a school at his ranch home on Hubbard Creek and invited his neighbors to send their children to this frontier institution. Young Johnnie Ledbetter was one of the pupils enrolled and, living too far to ride horseback each day, was taken into the Lynch home to board.

One afternoon Johnnie slipped away from the Lynch home so quietly that he was not missed until almost night. Perhaps he was simply bored with school and the confinement indoors. The search was started immediately. A courier hastened to the Ledbetter home with the disturbing news and then rode on to other ranches to get as many men as possible to join the searching party. A rider was sent to Fort Griffin, established in 1867, to secure aid in finding the boy. The Tonkawa trailers from the fort located Comanche pony tracks and the party took up the trail, followed it some distance, but were never able to overtake the raiders.

No positive trace of Johnnie Ledbetter was ever found. He had simply disappeared. Had the Indians stolen him and taken him out of the country? Had the Indians killed the boy and hidden his body? Or, had he simply become lost and, like numerous others, perished somewhere in the vast uncharted wilderness? "Quien Sabe!" The sorrowing parents never gave up hope and were ever alert to follow any clue concerning their lost son. Years went by and no trace or tidings concerning Johnnie Ledbetter were reported.

    The sequel to the story culminated finally in local tradition and legend. One account (C. C. Rister, *Fort Griffin on the Texas Frontier*) relates that nine years later a bronzed, unkempt youth came to Fort Griffin to sell a wagonload of buffalo hides. He said that he came from the Palo Duro Canyon country in the Texas Panhandle. It is told that the Ledbetters questioned the boy, who said that he had been stolen by the Indians and later bartered to a renegade white man who kept the boy on the Staked Plains. It is also told that the boy never lived with the Ledbetters but went to San Antonio and lived there until his death. It was true that Fort Griffin was at one time the headquarters of buffalo hunters and a booming market for buffalo hides.

    Fort Griffin was also a booming cowtown on the Western Cattle Trail, with ample saloons and general merchandise stores to meet the needs of the lusty cowboys who drove the herds of Texas Longhorns to Kansas. Another story (John C. Jacobs, "The Mysterious Ledbetter Boy," in *Frontier Times,* Vol. 4, No. 7; April 1927) is that a young cowboy about seventeen years old was with one of the trail herds near Fort Griffin when he was injured by an outlaw horse. The Jacksons, a ranch family, took the boy into their home and cared for him until he recovered. When asked his name, the boy replied that "Buckskin Bob" was the only name he knew. The Jacksons' interest in the boy brought out his story. He said that Indians had carried him into the Devil's River country and traded him to a peculiar frontier character, a white man named Tiger Jim. He could recall that he had ridden horseback with the Indians for a long distance and that they tied him to a stake every night. Tiger Jim gave a pony and a pistol in exchange for the boy. Tiger Jim, by use of the Bible and the dictionary, had taught the boy to read and write but the latter had been more interested in riding horseback and in hunting. When Bob was nearly grown, Old Tiger Jim went away to get supplies and left the boy alone. The boy decided that he would explore some. He saddled his pony and, with his rifle and pistol and a few rations, started riding toward the northeast. He rode mostly at night and kept a keen lookout for Indians. Finally he came to a ranch on the Concho River where the cowboys were rounding up a herd of cattle to drive up the trail to Kansas. Buckskin Bob became a cowboy—and enjoyed every minute of it—until the horse crippled him near Fort Griffin.

Mrs. Jackson knew the story of the missing Ledbetter boy of course and she arranged for the Ledbetter parents to meet Buckskin Bob. The mother was fully convinced that the boy was her son, but the father was not certain. Numerous points of circumstantial evidence bore out the mother's belief, including a certain scar on the boy's body where he had been "branded" by his playmates at one time. The boy went home with the Ledbetters, to live with them as a member of the family.

But Buckskin Bob had led a life too free and wild to be hampered by family ties and obligations. He soon chafed at ordinary, every-day life on a ranch. There was no excitement and no roaming the country at will. One morning he was missing. The story continues that the boy went to the Indian territory, stole a bunch of ponies, and drove them back to Texas and sold them. He was caught—and was fortunate enough to get a trial. He was brought before a judge who knew the Ledbetter family and the history of the boy. The judge turned him loose after the boy promised to go straight. The boy then went to Galveston and by tramp steamer made his way to South America, where he stayed a year. Returning to Texas, Buckskin Bob was converted to religion by a noted evangelist and in time the boy became a preacher.

Years later Buckskin Bob, now a noted evangelist himself, wrote to Mrs. Ledbetter from Ohio stating that he had found evidence that caused him to believe that he was not the Ledbetter boy. Another boy named Wesley had been stolen by the Indians about the same time, and Bob believed that he was that boy. He thanked Mrs. Ledbetter for her kindness and vowed he would ever remember her as a mother. She still believed that he was her son.

What became of Johnnie Ledbetter?

## 30. Bosque John Learned The White Man's Ways

American Indians in general were slow to adopt the white man's civilization, as well as his brand of salvation. Especially did the savage horseman of the western plains show indifference to his white brother's way of life. The nomadic red man was not reluctant, however, when it came to appropriating the horses of some frontier settler, lifting the owner's scalp, or taking his children or even his wife into captivity. The glittering gee-gaws and the firewater of the trader might attract his childlike fancies but seldom was the Indian caught in showing much visible, active interest in the white man's vaunted progress and inventions.

A case in point, where Indian curiosity intrigued the whole tribe, was the time when Bosque John was sent into Austin, frontier capital of the young Republic of Texas, by his Keechi Indian tribesmen, to verify some unbelievable stories which the Comanches had told them. This band of Comanches, after a raid into unprotected Austin, said that the whites "lived in houses that light shone through"; that from the outside one could watch the whites eating and drinking inside the house; and, that this strange magic material shut out sound and wind but did not interfere with sight.

Now, Bosque John thought that he was all Indian and in training to become a full-fledged Keechi warrior. Actually, he had been born John McLennan and had been kidnapped when very young. Perhaps that was why the Keechi chose him to play the lead in the adventure story which Bosque John told to his Texas Ranger companions in later years.

As John recalled it, a roving band of Comanches visited the Keechi village and recounted strange tales about what they had recently seen on a brief raid into Austin. So fantastic were some of the descriptions, that the Keechi secretly doubted the whole thing and believed that the Comanches were telling big lies. The Keechi were so intrigued with the glass windows idea that they called a council after the Comanches had moved on. They deliberated at length on some way to check the truth of the story. They selected Bosque John to go alone into Austin to act as a spy for the Keechi. The Indians knew that he was a white boy and perhaps this influenced their choice.

A small party of riders accompanied the boy on the trip to the very outskirts of Austin and sent John on his mission afoot. He slipped in after dark, gliding from one shadow to another. He soon realized that the Comanches had not lied. He came to a saloon, with wide front windows. He crept as near as he dared, flattened his body against the building, and peered intently through the glass. He saw men drinking and gambling. He knew that the men were talking but could not hear what they said. He gazed intently on the scene for some time, so absorbed that he forgot everything else. He placed his hand on this strange material which stopped all sound and even stopped the wind. He was fascinated by the looks and actions of the white men but he was puzzled and felt a rising resentment against these intruders into his people's homeland. He backed away from the window. Suddenly, without knowing why, he drew his bow and sent an arrow against the smooth, clear surface.

The crash of breaking, falling glass was like thunder in the stillness of the night. The boy turned and ran for his life. He did not stop until he reached his companions.

John's report to his tribesmen created wonder and much talk. The old men of the tribe pointed out that the

Indian was doomed, that he could not hold out against a race of men who could create such things as "houses that the light shone through." The Keechi chiefs were ready to make a treaty with the whites.

The first treaty with the whites was made on Tehuacana Creek in 1844. The Keechi and numerous other tribes met with representatives of the Republic of Texas in a grand council. The white men noted especially one young brave among the Keechi. He was much taller than his companions. His skin was sun-browned but was considerably lighter than the Indians. His hair was not Indian black, but auburn. Some of the Rangers tried to talk to the boy but he responded only with a sullen glare. In no way did he show that he understood a word of English.

The next year, another great council was held. The Keechi were called upon to give up their white captive. The wily Keechi chief, venerable Saatzarook, rose and made a long oration, entirely ignoring the demand. The white commissioner pointedly asked why the white boy had not been brought to the pow-wow. At length, after much humming and hawing, the chief offered the excuse that the boy had no horse to ride but if the whites would furnish the horse, the boy would be brought in. The whites knew that all this was meant to delay the showdown. It was common knowledge that these Indians were notorious horse thieves, usually with a large herd of horses in their possession. When the council ended, ten Texas Rangers were sent to the Keechi camp to bring in the boy. The old chief objected to the last, telling the Rangers that the boy was not only his very best warrior but also he was "one fine horse-thief."

The young white brave did not want to leave the Indians. He was ready to fight or run. Some of the other young men of the tribe came to his rescue and strung their bows. The old chief restored order and began to harangue the boy. He told the boy that he was white, and that according to the treaty he was to go to his relatives. If he did not like the new life, he could always run away and return to the Keechi. The Rangers quickly took the boy away, before he could escape or the old chief could change his mind.

The young Indianized white boy had been born John McLennan, in a log cabin on the Brazos River not far from present Waco. The McLennan brothers,—Neil, John, and

Laughlin—had settled on the Indian frontier in 1835. In that year, a band of Keechi had swooped down upon the Laughlin McLennan's cabin, killed the father and grandmother, and carried off the wife and three children. Mrs. McLennan and her young daughter died on the flight from the cabin. One young son was traded off and the older boy, then about six, was adopted by the Keechi, an old woman in the tribe becoming his foster-mother. He grew up thinking he was an Indian. He spent his formative years with the Keechi in their nomadic moves over a range teeming with such game as buffalo, antelope and deer. It was a care-free life he loved.

Now, the fifteen year-old boy was uprooted from this life. The weather was cold and the Rangers put a shirt and pants on the boy. He quickly pulled off the shirt and cut the pants so as to make leggings. When the party reached Torrey's trading house John was still typical Indian in appearance and he was scornful of what he saw of the white man's ways.

Indian agent Len H. Williams believed that the boy was John Parker, brother of Cynthia Ann Parker. He wrote to Isaac Parker, uncle of the kidnapped Parker children, asking him to come and take the boy in charge. On December 30, 1845, however, Williams reported that Neil McLennan, for whom the Texas county was named, had definitely identified the boy as his nephew and had taken him in charge.

Thus the bewildered young Indian brave became, at least partially and at times, John McLennan. He found himself rich for those days. His uncle had taken care of his father's land and herd of cattle. The Texas Legislature granted John a league of land—4,428 acres. But he could never forget his Indian life and it was a rough road to change to the white man's ways.

The first night at his uncle's home, John refused to enter the house but stood all night under a tree, holding to the mane of his pony. He never slept in a regular bed but gradually he adjusted to his new environment.

Bosque John joined the Texas Rangers and served under Captain Sul Ross. His training as an Indian was of great help in tracking down Indian horse thieves. John told the Rangers many of his experiences while with the Indians.

In time John settled down and married and raised a family. He developed his rich lands and looked after his cattle and horses. But when his Indian friends came to visit, he dropped everything and went on long hunts with them. His wife sometimes doubted that he would ever return.

John avoided crowds whenever possible. When he had to go into the village of Waco to spend the night, he would sleep on the floor of the second story in the county courthouse. One night, in 1866, he walked through one of the large glass windows and broke his neck in the fall to the ground. Thus the white man's glass had special significance in his life. His remains today lie in an unmarked grave somewhere along the Bosque River.

## 31. Coryell Youth Had Brief Ride With Brutal Redskins

In 1864, the ten-year-old son of Captain Gideon Graham of Coryell County was sent by his mother to drive in the horses, which were grazing near the house. A party of lurking Indians, hiding in the brush, captured the boy and fled with him and all the horses. The marauders were seen by Captain Burleson, a neighbor of the Grahams, who quickly raised a pursuit party and managed to get near enough to fire at the retreating thieves. The Indians were thrown into confusion and scattered in the brush.

The Graham lad saw a chance to escape and tried to jump from his horse. A burly savage grabbed him by the arm and the wild ride continued. The chase soon became so hot that the Indian decided to drop the boy but, as he did so, he brutally thrust his lance entirely through the little fellow's body.

Captain Burleson came upon the fallen lad and saw that he was alive. Some of the men carried the bleeding boy to the nearest house. Mrs. Graham was brought to her son and nursed him back to health.

## 32. Texas Ranger Had Been A Comanche Captive For Ten Years

Warren Lyons, Texas Ranger under such redoubtable leaders as Rip Ford and Ed Burleson, had spent ten years apprenticeship as a captive and a warrior with the nomadic Comanches. His skill and training thus acquired proved to be most helpful to the Rangers in their attempt to protect the Texas frontier against Comanche raiders.

Early one morning, the thirteen-year-old Warren and his father were in the cowpen milking. The other members of the family were still asleep. Without any warning whatever some thirty Comanches, seeking revenge for losses in a recent fight, suddenly surrounded the pen. The father was killed and scalped. Warren, although unarmed, put up a valiant fight but was seized by a burly rider and pulled up on the back of a horse. The Indians quickly rounded up the Lyons' horses and fled the scene before the other members of the family were aroused. Neighbors of the Lyons in the La Grange area followed the trail but to no avail.

Thus began the white boy's ten eventful years with "the lords of the plains," the far-riding Comanches. Diligent efforts were made to find the boy but only vague rumors resulted. Only the mother clung to the belief that her son, the baby in the family, was still alive and she prayed constantly for his return.

German scientist Ferdinand Roemer in his book, *Texas,* recorded his observations concerning Warren Lyons

in his Indian habitat. Roemer, with Robert S. Neighbors, Indian agent, and Jim Shaw, the Delaware interpreter, went to the Comanche camp on the San Saba River, in February of 1847, where they met John Meusebach and some of his German settlers from Fredericksburg in council with the Comanches. Roemer saw a blue-eyed, blond youth, with all the Anglo Saxon characteristics, dressed in the usual Comanche style. Jim Shaw, Delaware interpreter, well versed in Indian lore, told Roemer that the boy was Warren Lyons, that he was about 18 years old, and had been with the Indians for some ten years. The Indians had killed the boy's father and Warren thought they had killed his mother also. Now he was an Indian in everything except appearance. He could not be persuaded to visit his brother near Austin. Comanche like, he distrusted all whites.

Roemer was greatly interested in noting that Warren had acquired a small Mexican boy, about eight years of age, who apparently was treated as a slave. The boy was half-starved in appearance, scantily clad, and was shivering in the cold north February wind as he sat behind Warren on horseback. This boy excited Roemer's pity and with Jim Shaw's aid questioned Warren about the Mexican boy. Warren showed the usual Comanche contempt for the Mexicans by stating, in an arrogant manner, that he had caught the boy on the Rio Grande. Roemer understood this to mean about the same as catching a wild horse.

The full story of Warren's experiences with the Indians is not available but it is safe to say that he came to love the adventurous roving life on horseback. In typical fashion, he learned to ride as only a Comanche boy could, to use the bow and arrow, and to fight. We do know that ten years after his capture Warren had become a full-fledged Comanche warrior, thoroughly Indian in everything except his appearance.

In 1847, during the Mexican War, a party of Comanches made one of their periodic visits to San Antonio to barter and to see the white man's sights. Two neighbors of the Lyons family were in the Alamo City at the time and they noticed that one of the young warriors had most of the characteristics of a white and, more important, that he resembled the Lyons brothers so much that they decided that he might be Warren Lyons, now twenty-three. Through an interpreter they secured enough information to become certain. By patient haggling, considerable diplomacy, and with the giving of numerous presents, they arranged to take the young warrior home. Warren objected strenuously—he did not want to go. He believed that his mother was dead. Also, he had acquired two young wives and he had no reason whatever to abandon them or the way of life he had come to love. Finally, a gift of a new red blanket to each wife led him to promise to go with the neighbors on a visit to his mother, with the understanding that he would then return to his wives and his tribe. In full Indian garb, he accompanied the two men to his old home.

Warren recognized his mother at once and put on such a demonstration that his parent was almost unnerved, since she did not at first know her son. But the reunion proved to be joyful—the mother trying to hold the Indian warrior in her arms, while he showed his delight by dancing about and making gutteral sounds in Indian fashion.

Dan W. Roberts, noted Texas Ranger Captain, furnished a somewhat different version of the restoration of Warren Lyons to his family. He stated that he was a small boy at the time but would never forget that he was at the Lyons' home in Lavaca County when the reunion took place. James B. Roberts, uncle of the Ranger Captain, when locating land for the Germans near Fredericksburg, visited the Comanche camp on Honey Creek near present Mason. He saw and talked with a young white warrior and decided that he was no doubt Warren Lyons. The young man seemed anxious to return home when he found that his mother was alive and at the old home. The two made arrangements for several men to meet Warren in San Antonio when the Comanches went there to trade the next time.

Captain Roberts asserted that Warren had not forgotten the English language and when he reached home talked freely. The hair on one side of his head had been cut very short. Warren told his listeners that this was his punishment for running away in a fight which the Comanches had with the Mexicans a short time before.

Warren fully expected to return to his Comanche wives but it seemed that all his family and neighbors were in a giant conspiracy to detain him on one pretense after another. Finally, he agreed to accompany his brother,

Dewitt, and join a Ranger company to fight the Mexicans, whom the Comanches hated.

Thus the Indian warrior joined the Texan side and became acquainted with Rangers who were also expert horsemen and fighters. It was not too long before the Ranger company was pitted against Comanche raiders. Gradually Warren was weaned away from his Indian ways and habits so that he became more like his brothers. While in the Ranger force he was in several fights with the Indians, and also served as guide and interpreter. When the Rangers fought the Comanches, Warren always pulled his boots off, jumped about, dodged, and changed positions so as to present a more difficult target.

Later, Warren married and settled down near the old family home.

## 33.  Young Woman From Texas

A disheveled white woman, riding alone and bareback on a shaggy pony, jarred Bob Bent loose from the last smidgen of his usual taciturnity. This happened one morning in 1865 on the Old Santa Fe Trail. Bob Bent, half-Cheyenne son of old plainsman, Bill Bent, was not one easily surprised. This seasoned frontiersman was "tough as chawed leather," in parlance of the frontier. But as he led his plodding wagon train near the Arkansas River, the apparition of a solitary white woman, hundreds of miles from civilization, astounded him—and he showed it.

A closer look showed that the woman was utterly exhausted and about to fall from the pony's back. Her hair was uncombed, her dress torn and soiled. Her eyes reflected an ordeal of past suffering. Bent and his teamsters quickly gave her food and water. After she had eaten, Bent questioned her.

"Where did you come from?"

"Texas," was the laconic reply.
"Who are you?"
"Mary Jane Roberts."
"And how did you get this far from home?"

With the dusty teamsters encircling her, Mrs. Roberts tersely unfolded a tale of bloodshed, horror and tears—the nightmare of her back trail to her home in Wise County, Texas.

The young widow, about twenty-two, was staying in the home of John S. Babb when suddenly forty yelling Comanches surrounded the cabin. The father was not at home. Dot Babb, thirteen and a tried frontiersman, with the help of his mother and Mrs. Roberts barred the door. The Indians quickly broke this down, murdered Mrs. Babb and her infant, seized Mrs. Roberts, nine-year-old Bianca

Babb, her brother Dot, and quickly dragged the captives to waiting horses outside. An eternity of horror was compressed into those few moments of fiendish bloodshed for the three captives. The savages beat the helpless three with their quirts as they mounted each behind an Indian horseman.

Then began a horseback ride of nearly a thousand miles—a trail of tears, sheer human torture, and prolonged suffering. The painted brutes, as usual, rode day and night as fast as their horses could carry them—no food, no rest, no sleep—only occasional brief halts until after the Red River had been crossed. The suffering whites were guarded constantly but finally were able to make plans for escape. Mrs. Roberts, being a real judge of horses picked two horses and Dot was to picket the animals in a certain spot one night. The captives knew that the chief had picked the young woman as his squaw and decided that death was preferable. But the plan did not pan out. Dot was caught before he reached his horse. His sister was unable to slip from her bed.

Mary Jane Roberts caught her horse, straddled him bareback, and slowly walked him away from the Indian camp. There was no moon. With unflagging spirit she guided her mount toward the north star, depressed by having to abandon the Babb children to their savage captors but buoyed by her own release, the awful fate of a white woman captive being an oft-repeated warning all along the frontier. Her mind was made up to escape and try to ransom the children later.

All night the intrepid Mary Jane rode hard. She had picked a good horse and the noble animal served her heroically. During the next day she pushed on, hungry, dead-tired, and groggy from loss of sleep. The second night a pack of wolves caught up, even snapping at the heels of the played-out horse. Finally, after daylight, the wolves gave up the chase. The tired rider slid from the pony's back to the ground and was instantly in a deep sleep.

Hours later she was awakened by the sound of horses' hoofs. She sat up and saw mounted Indians surrounding her. She jumped to her feet. Some of the savages now dismounted, pressing around her, brandishing tomahawks and uttering diabolical yells. Mary Jane weakened by her grueling ordeals of captivity and starvation, knew that she faced death. Mercifully she fainted. After she recovered, the Indians placed her upon a horse and rode with her to their nearby camp. The prisoner was turned over to the squaws, who gave her food and let her sleep and rest. It was several days before she could walk. She learned that her captors were Kiowas, belonging to Lone Wolf's band. Again she was doomed to marry a chief and was placed in charge of an old squaw. She vowed not to become a slave for life.

Mrs. Roberts had no remote idea as to her location or the direction of the nearest white settlement. One party of Kiowa warriors headed north from camp one morning and returned six days later with some ears of green corn. This clue gave her hope and speeded her escape.

Late one night the desperate captive stole from the lodge where she was guarded, made her stealthy way to the horse herd, and had caught a pony when the pack of camp dogs set up a bedlam of barking. She hastily gave up her plan and crawled back to her bed undetected. In her second attempt, the omens were favorable. A few nights later she caught an excellent horse and rode northward, guided by the stars and the sun. For three days and nights she rode rapidly, resting her horse occasionally.

In due time Mrs. Roberts reached the Arkansas River. It was at flood stage and the torrent was swift and powerful. The dauntless woman did not hesitate but rode her tired horse into foaming water. With much urging and encouragement from the rider, the noble animal landed safely on the opposite bank. Giving her mount a short rest, she moved forward.

She rode only a short distance from the river when she

found a broad, wheel-marked wagon road. Her joy knew no bounds. It was the first and only evidence of civilization since leaving Wise County weeks before. Her stoical fortitude, which had borne her unfalteringly through every hazard, deserted her entirely when she saw a long wagon train approaching at some distance across the prairie. She wept with joy and offered thanks to the Almighty for her deliverance from a bondage more dreaded than death.

Bob Bent and his incredulous bull-whackers listened to Mrs. Roberts with awe. They simply could not believe her story, which she spent less time in telling than you have spent in reading. Bent expected the woman to ride with his wagons to the nearest settlement. But she thanked Bent, mounted her pony, and rode away. Some miles later she luckily met some United States soldiers who, upon hearing her story, escorted her to Council Grove, Kansas. Here she met a family whom she accompanied to their home. She afterward married a prosperous stockman named Van Noy. The couple settled in Galena, Kansas, and raised a large family. Mary Jane died in Galena in 1904.

After nearly two years of captivity the unhappy Babb children were ransomed from their captors by their father. Dot Babb, after a full and eventful life, when an old man, wrote an account of his experiences. His book, entitled *In The Bosom Of The Comanches,* pays tribute to the courage of Mrs. Luster, as he called her.

The story of indomitable Mary Jane Roberts and her perilous ride became an unforgotten chronicle of the frontier.

BIBLIOGRAPHY and FOOTNOTES

1. Smith, Clinton L. & Jefferson D., *The Boy Captives,* 1927; and *The San Antonio Express,* April 22, 1940.
2. Hunter's *Frontier Times,* Bandera, Texas, October 1927 and September 1954; and Ole T. Nystel, *Three Months With The Comanches,* 1888.
3. Hunter's *Frontier Times,* Bandera, Texas 1944.
4. *The Fort Worth Press,* April 1, 1936; and *Frontier Times,* Vol. 8, No. 2.
5. T. A. (Dott) Babb, *In The Bosom Of The Comanches,* 1912.

6. Clarence R. Wharton, *Satanta (Kiowa Chief)*, 1935.
7. A. J. Sowell, *Texas Indian Fighters*, 1900.
8. Hunter's *Frontier Times*, Bandera, May, 1935; and *Memorial And Genealogical Record of Southwest Texas*, 1894.
9. C. C. Rister, *Border Captives*, 1956.
10. *Frontier Times*, no date.
11. A. J. Sowell, *Early Settlers and Indian Fighters In Southwest Texas;* Day & Winfrey, *Texas Indian Papers, 1860-1916;* and J. Marvin Hunter, *History of Bandera County*, 1922.
12. *Frontier Times*, no date.
13. *The Abilene Reporter*, Abilene, Texas, September 1928.
14. Personal interviews with Acie Adams, Killeen, Texas.
15. Herman Lehmann, *Nine Years Among The Indians*, 1927.
16. Hugh D. Corwin, *Comanche And Kiowa Captives*, 1959 and W. S. Nye, *Carbine and Lance*, 1942.
17. *The Cattleman*, Fort Worth, Texas, April 1944.
18. Hugh D. Corwin, *Comanche And Kiowa Captives*, 1959.
19. Colonel Richard I. Dodge, *33 Years Among Our Wild Indians*, 1959 edition.
20. *Texas Indian Papers, 1860-1916* and Hugh D. Corwin, *Comanche And Kiowa Captives*.
21. Hunter's *Frontier Times*, July 1927 and *Texas Indian Papers, 1846-1859*.
22. John H. Brown, *Indian Wars And Pioneers In Texas* and Grant Foreman, *Advancing The Frontier*, 1933.
23. T. R. Havins, *Something About Brown* (County), 1958 and J. M. Franks, *Sixty Years In Texas*.
24. John M. Elkins, *Indian Fighting On The Texas Frontier*, 1928 and T. R. Havins, *Something About Brown* (County).
25. C. C. Rister, *Border Captives* and *Texas Indian Papers, 1860-1916*.
26. George W. Tyler, *History of Bell County*, 1966.
27. Hunter's *Frontier Times*, June 1927; Greg Olds, "Effects of the 1839 Webster Massacre on Burnet's Founding," *The Highlander*, Marble Falls, Texas, December 23, 1971; and, T. R. Fehrenbach, *The Comanches*, 1974.
28. C. C. Rister, *Fort Girffin on the Texas Frontier*, 1956 and Hunter's *Frontier Times*, April 1927.
29. Same as above.
30. Winfrey, *Texas Indian Papers, 1844-1845* and for 1846-1859.
31. Mildred W. Mears, *Coryell County Scrapbook*.
32. Hunter's *Frontier Times;* Ferdinand Roemer, *Texas, 1967; and Dan W. Roberts, Rangers and Sovereignty*, 1914.
33. T. A. (Dot) Babb, *In The Bosom Of The Comanches;* Shannon Garth, *William Bent*, 1957; and *Texas Indian Papers 1860-1916*.